The Big Book of Homeschooling
Copyright © Michael and Debi Pearl

ISBN: 978-1-61644-068-8
January 2014

Visit www.NoGreaterJoy.org for information on this and other products produced by No Greater Joy Ministries

Requests for information should be addressed to:
No Greater Joy Ministries Inc.
1000 Pearl Road
Pleasantville, TN 37033
USA

All scripture quotations are taken from the King James Holy Bible.

Written by Debi Pearl
Illustrations, Photography, and Interior layout design by Erin Harrison

The BIG Book of Homeschooling

Learn From Veteran Homeschool Mama
and International Best Selling Author

Debi Pearl

Acknowledgements

A big **THANK YOU** to all the homeschooling moms
who contributed stories or ideas to this volume.
It is your creativity, passion and hard work,
along with your love and sacrifice for your children
that made it possible.

I also want to thank Mike, my husband, and all five of our children
whose articles I pulled from http://nogreaterjoy.org
Their insights fit so well our subject of homeschooling.

Thanks to Bobbie Sue Johnson,
my energetic organizer and motivator,
for the resource pages.

And last, thanks to my proofers—
Mike, Jared, and Aaron.
(You can blame them.)

Debi

Contents

Volume 32, Number 13 — Millington, Tennessee — 25 cents

Teaching at home

Home education of children is a rule followed in the Michael and Debi Pearl home in the Shelby Forest area. Mrs. Pearl [above] spends several hours a day with their children helping them with lessons. The couple is currently joining other such families across the state in a battle to guarantee the rights of parents to educate children at home.

[Mark Price photo]

Couple fights for right to educate kids at home

The Vision

The homeschooling movement started in the early 1970s with families who independently conceived of the idea. Thinking they were alone in their vision, they withheld their children from the public mills and started quietly teaching them at home. I know because I was there; I was one of those who had a dream. As far as I knew we were the only family that had ever dared teach our children at home. Then the thing we feared came upon us. The Department of Child Services showed up at our door saying we were breaking the law and were in danger of losing our children to "the system." Whoa! Nothing seemed scarier than having our children taken from us and placed in a godless home. Life can really throw some curves. We made plans to flee the country, to seek freedom and liberty in some third-world jungle.

At that time, there were no support groups or legal services dedicated to helping radical parents who dared challenge truancy laws. Parents and friends were not sympathetic or supportive. It was scary knowing we were all alone in this quest of raising and educating our children the way God commanded.

One day, after leaving the judge's chambers under threat of removing our children from our home, we walked down the hall to the office of a state senator, who was a friend, and told him of our predicament. He said we should call the newspapers and TV stations with the spin that the city of Memphis was trying to prevent us from giving our children a more advanced form of education. He told us to demand that our children be tested before they determined us to be unfit as teachers.

The media had never heard of homeschooling and saw it as an exciting story of the little man versus the big, insensitive establishment. We entertained news reporters and photographers from both print media and TV. Mike clearly and forcefully asserted the God-given right to raise our children free from the ungodly influences of public school and to give them a quality education. Suddenly, we were on TV and in multi-page spreads in the local newspapers, being called to testify before the authorities, and taking our children to be tested by hostile teachers. We became an overnight, infamous oddity. Our phone began to ring off the wall; the callers were other families who were also secretly homeschooling their children, thinking they were the only ones doing this "weird" thing.

All of these families shared a dream of taking charge of their own lives, hopes, and destinies. Homeschooling did not begin as a top-down master plan, urged upon the populace by someone with a political or social agenda. It began with God moving in the hearts of many parents, waking them to the need to put their families first and lead the charge away from the evil that our society was quickly moving toward. These bold parents aggressively called their children to follow them into victory. At the beginning, for most of these pioneers, it was a clash with the school system, courts, extended family (the hardest), and the church. Notable church leaders said we "should obey the law"—send our children to the public schools.

It was this very struggle that made the pioneer homeschooling families so successful both in education and in life. All truly successful families share a dream and each member pours their energies into making it a reality. After a decade, the battle for the right to homeschool was won. No one told the children that they were part of a bigger picture—changing the world to one where homeschooling was not only legal, it was also normal—and soon thousands of children would follow their lead. They, like their parents, picked up the mantle and wore it with distinction.

Here we are 40 years later. Everyone in the country knows the words "home schooling," now one word—homeschooling. Over two million children are homeschooled, and the number increases every year. There is an industry of homeschooling materials, curriculum fairs with thousands in attendance, and homeschooled kids winning national spelling bees and science fairs. You can now

contract an attorney who was homeschooled, or go to a doctor who did his K through 12 in his home with Mom as the teacher. Many scientists, musicians, and politicians attribute their success to mom and dad and the kitchen table. Best of all, homeschoolers have found each other and formed tens of thousands of beautiful marriages based on virtue and a vision of passing the torch to the next generation.

The early homeschooling pioneers were people of conviction. They chose a path from which there was no retreat, expecting good things from their efforts, and few were disappointed. But the movement has since strayed from its roots. It has been institutionalized and codified in a manner that leaves no room for vision and individual expression. Homeschoolers have adopted the techniques of corporate education, assuming the nature of a small, isolated, public classroom. The glowing reports of homeschool successes, the made-to-order curriculum, the support system, and the glamour of independent action have drawn in many who have no conviction and would never have endured the early days of homeschooling. In the early days, homeschooling was built on a vision that was not written down and for which there was no measure. For that reason we hear reports of some parents growing weary and throwing in the towel, putting their kids in public school or an equally destructive "Christian" school.

Are you on the verge of giving up? Are you frustrated and weary with the process? Are your children discontent? Before you give your children over to be educated by a system that is anti-God and anti-decency, consider the fact that not all homeschooling is created equal. It was a whole lot more fun in the early days—fun for the kids *and* the parents. This book is written to free you from the bondage of what has now become the tradition of homeschooling. I want to help you be a pioneer in your own home, just like we were when there was no one telling us how it should be done, when we were free to dream, to have a vision, to be creative, and to do our own thing.

I have recounted this history because one of the most necessary but largely missing elements of successfully homeschooling children and raising them to be strong, confident leaders is a vision. In this book I will teach you about vision and give you a number of examples of people with vision who have proven to be extremely successful, as seen in the fruit of their now-grown children and grandchildren.

Observing this erosion of early homeschooling principles, early in 2002 I sent out an appeal to successful homeschooling families to share their "tried-and-proven" experiences and methods. I received hundreds of fascinating letters, many from the early pioneers whose children were by then already grown. We have personally known many families whose children became outstanding missionaries, scientists, doctors, lawyers, national security intelligence analysts, and honest laborers contributing to society.

Are you on the verge of giving up? Are you frustrated and weary with the process? Are your children discontent?

But then, right in the middle of collating these fascinating letters which were loaded with so many wonderfully crazy ideas, my husband had a major life-threatening heart attack. Nothing else in this life seems very important when things like that happen. Yet, on the way to the hospital, while in the clutches of horrific pain, he told our oldest son, "Gabe, I am giving your mama one last duty as my wife. She is to write the book for ladies on how to have a good marriage. She has planned on doing it for years but has been distracted serving me; now is the time. It will be called 'Created to Be His Help Meet.'" He barely survived the heart attack, but didn't forget my errand (he is still alive and kicking higher than ever). Within days after we got home from the hospital, he set up an office for me in my parents' empty vacation home and told me I was to be there at 6 AM each morning and could come home at 6 PM in the evening. He would bring my meals and hand them in through the door.

From the time I was 13 years old, I had kept notes from preachers, teachers, books, pamphlets, and even conversations. I had a huge box of musty old papers to resource and put into a file on the computer. Forced into the silence with just a computer (and no internet), I quickly began the task. Within three weeks the notes were entered and organized into book form. My husband began editing, and in short order *Created to Be His Help Meet* hit the market.

The immediate success of the book took us all by surprise and it completely stole my urgency to write the homeschooling book that had so captivated my mind before the heart attack. Suddenly I had become an international bestselling author; I was busy, busy, busy. Several books on the same subject followed. The homeschooling book fell by the wayside.

I want to help you be a pioneer in your own home, just like we were when there was no on telling us how it should be done.

Now, 11 years later, it has become apparent that the need for a homeschooling revival is greater than ever. So, about a year ago, I decided to revive the project and sent out a fresh appeal for best homeschooling ideas. Many responded and I was shocked at the difference 10 years could make. The freshness and creativity was gone. In its place was concern for this curriculum versus that work book or pace. I read their frustration and anxiety. Many were concerned about their discontented children and their own hardships. Families are yielding to a system that has evolved by default, giving up their creativity for institutionalized school at home. The kids continue to surpass their public school peers and are being protected from the corruption, but many are not experiencing the excitement and thrill that the liberty of homeschooling affords. So, I approach this book with a great deal of hope. I am hoping to free you from the shackles of what other people think and what convention says, and to give you permission to chart your own course and be daring in your approach to schooling your children at home.

The decade-long delay was providential, for at that time homeschooling parents were not ready to accept criticism of the developing system propagated by so many wise men and women. But time is a test that tells the truth about our methods and beliefs. Until now, the world was not ready for *The BIG Book of Homeschooling*. Time has worked its sifting process, having either exposed weakness or placed its stamp of approval upon our varied methods. The large number of homeschooled children, now grown and having children of their own, has yielded laboratory-quality results that identify the best approaches to homeschooling. Yes, time has a way of proving or disproving a method that no amount of theorizing can gainsay.

Of Paramount Importance

Those of us who originally dared to take on the responsibility of educating our children at home were driven more by a desire to maintain control of the impartation of our Christian culture than by a desire for academic excellence. We took seriously the Biblical admonition to "Train up a child in the way he should go…."

"Whom shall he teach knowledge? and whom shall he make to understand doctrine? them that are weaned from the milk, and drawn from the breasts. For

Time has a way of proving or disproving a theory that no amount of theorizing can gainsay.

precept must be upon precept, precept upon precept; line upon line, line upon line; here a little, and there a little" (Isaiah 28:9-10).

We understood that more is caught than taught, that if we turned our children over to the public sector to work their agenda, we were throwing them into a hungry machine designed to impart everything that is contrary to all that is sacred and holy. We cared so dearly for the souls of our children that we could not surrender to the public sector those eight hours each day.

"For what is a man profited, if he shall gain the whole world, and lose his own soul? or what shall a man give in exchange for his soul?" (Matthew 16:26).

Likewise, what does it profit parents if their children gain a public education but lose their souls to the world, the flesh, and the devil? We early pioneers were possessed of a consuming conviction that would have forced us to flee the country or live in a cave before we would wed our children to the enemy of truth and righteousness. Yet today, conditions in the public schools are far more advanced toward the sins of Sodom and the garbage of Gomorra. Public schools are a homogenizing machine, designed to blend all ideas into one smooth, digestible, leftist agenda, rendered palatable to a gullible public.

"The three Rs" along with the sciences and music are only a small part of the education we wish to instill. At the time we started homeschooling, we had not formulated our views and would not have said that we were taking responsibility to pass on our Christian culture—but that was exactly our motivation. Culture is handed down from one generation to the next, and it is the greater part of our concern. Today, homeschoolers are inundated with a wide range of techniques, from extremely intense workbooks or hours of video to skipping school and taking care of the horses. After many years, what fruit have the different methods borne? Are families happy? Are children growing up to be hardworking entrepreneurs? Is this generation of homeschoolers marrying in purity and seeing fruits of love, joy, and peace? Are our children being turned into high-paid professionals but losing their own souls? Who cares if you can read when you end up on the street doing drugs? What does it matter if you finish your Algebra and then go have an abortion? A history major who cuts herself and has thoughts of suicide will not make her parents proud. Bring out your fruit and justify your methods.

The most important time in the education of a child is their very first exposure to what might be called their "formal education." If the experience is good, they will want more of it; if it is painful, they will shun it like a skinned knee. Their attitude toward learning is based on their feelings about themselves. When a child perceives in their parent's attitude the importance of their performance in learning, they feel the pressure to please, to perform. If they fail to perform and sense any impatience or disappointment in their parents it reduces their self-image and causes them to feel inadequate. Those first feelings of failure are attached to the very concept of math, reading, spelling, or any academic endeavor. From that point forward, they resist going to that place where they feel poorly about themselves—a reflection of how they think others view them. Those self-condemning feelings cause an internal freeze-up when faced with the prospect of learning, and it truly does reduce their ability to learn. As

parents or teachers see them falling behind their peers, they become more impatient and pushy, demanding performance and imparting a sense of rejection. Time and "underperformance" exacerbates the cycle and it becomes a syndrome of intellectual stupidity as the child retreats to a safe place where there is no expectation of having to use the brain. A self-image of "I can't" is cemented and the character of the child is forever built as a wall of hardened stones. When a parent or teacher says, "teaching him is like pulling teeth," I know that the child feels like his teeth are being pulled when teachers are demanding he do what he "knows" he cannot.

I say again, by far the most important moments in the education of a child are those first experiences in what they perceive to be the beginning of their career as a student of the arts and sciences. For that reason it is far more important to give attention to the concept of learning rather than to the content. Don't think so much about what they are learning as how they are learning. We must first instill the love of learning, the confidence of learning, the reward of learning, and the fellowship of learning. What one loves one does often; what one hates is avoided. It is far better to have a child three years behind his peers who loves learning than one barely maintaining his grade level through much forced repetitive pain. The kid who loves learning, regardless of his IQ, will become a lifetime student of everything. The child constantly constrained to learn will cease his education the moment he is free from the intimidation.

Therefore, in this book you will read many examples of making learning fun. In many instances, the education is disguised as free time or family fellowship. I have seen children five to seven years old who were reading anything they wanted to read and counting money like a Wal-Mart checkout clerk, and when I asked what they did for school, they said, "Oh, I start next year." I am talking about homeschoolers, kids that have learned the basics and yet didn't even know they were already being schooled.

The personal testimonies you will read are examples of how to begin and continue the educational process in a manner that makes it full and fulfilling. In so doing, we are imparting something far more important than academic skills; we are instilling a mindset of success based on self-worth and personal confidence.

This single principle is the crowning jewel of homeschooling. Public schools gender a survival of the fittest, allowing a few students to rise to the top but relegating the vast majority to a life of mediocrity. Parents hold in their hands the souls of their children and are able to gently steer every one of them, as different as they may be, into a path of personal worth and success. Public schools and Christian schools, corporate classroom settings, produce a few successes and a number of failures. School at home by deeply concerned and committed parents produces success in every child, without exception. This book is designed to help you make the kind of choices that will guarantee success with all your children.

A self-image of "I can't" is cemented and the character of the child is forever built as a wall of hardened stones.

I have read thousands of letters. I have followed the progress from birth to their giving birth. I have counseled and listened and observed and analyzed and prayed and considered and made notes and discussed and around and around and back again. But this is not my story; it is your story.

I know that wisdom is found in the "tried-and-proven" experiences of many homeschooling parents. The vast majority of the examples you are about to read came to me in the form of letters from pioneer homeschooling moms who were forced to step up and make the homeschooling thing happen without the comfort of fairs and tons of options that are available today.

You have taught me. I have listened and weighed, and am now going to publish your story, your experiences. Theory aside; this is the tried-and-proven.

Pearl Kid #1

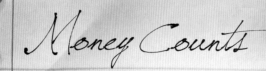

Money Counts

Behind Mom and Dad's door stood an old, five-gallon plastic jug, the origin of which I have long forgotten.

Every time Dad had a pocketful of small change, he would toss it into the jug behind the door. The five of us kids searched the laundry room, and even the street in front of the library for pennies and nickels to add to that old jug. It usually took about 6 months to get that jug about half full.

Finally, when we were convinced there was enough in there to make a difference, the three oldest of us would haul the jug to the table, heave it up, and dump it out. The shower of dirty change onto the table was a thrill I still vividly remember. Mom would hand us the bag of brown paper rolls from the bank, and the counting would begin. Even my three-year-old sister climbed up on the bench and counted out pennies. My six-year-old brother recounted her stacks, and my eight-year-old brother would recount next. And I, being the oldest, had to recount every stack just to make sure.

The first counting session was always a little disappointing. Our hopes were generally higher than the pile of change. But by the second or third counting, we triumphantly arrived at a figure that would take the whole family to Baskin Robbins for a banana split – EACH!

Looking back, I can't see much value in all the banana splits that once thrilled my heart, but counting that change, and recounting, and re-recounting was more valuable to my basic math skills than all Abeka math workbooks put together. We learned so much more than the value of a nickel.

All the universe is set up in number patterns.

The **Bible** is a series of number patterns.
Did you know that the book of Revelation
in the KJV has exactly **12,000** words?

Debi

 Websites and Resources for Phonics found on page 22-23

Brush up on your math skills with a fun game!

- Write math problems on note cards.
- Tape cards on Toss Across game.
- When you toss the bean bag on the card, you must say the answer to the problem.

Math for Beginners

The next few concepts, properly applied, could make a mathematician out of any kid. Many children don't do well in math simply because there is no association between the practical and the theoretical. It is through a variety of experiences that children come to conceptualize addition. Even crows can add and subtract. If three men walk into a barn next to a freshly planted corn field where crows are pulling up the little seeds, and two men leave while one hides in the barn, the crows will not return. They obviously know that three men minus two men leaves one shotgun in the barn. When the third man leaves, they again do some ciphering and return to the field. Smart crows. Children can add and subtract long before we try to theorize it on paper. If you don't think so, take three cookies and place them under a napkin. Give the two-year-old child one cookie, and after he eats it give him the second cookie, and then stop. You will see that he knows there is a third cookie still in the napkin. He is counting. If he can experience the practical and then see how it is represented on paper, he will immediately make the application. Teach real life math, then hand the child a workbook and he can go through several years' worth of workbooks in a month's time. If he can't immediately grasp the book math, do not keep pushing. Find a practical and interesting way to do the same thing in real life and continue until he can make the transition easily. When paper math serves a purpose that pleases the child, you are over the hump and in the winner's circle.

These Feet Were for Walking

Reflecting back: I bought a roll of pap[er] a line of numbers large enough that it could be "walked." I handed my 7-year-old his math book and showed him how to proceed.

He opened his math book to the page for the day and read aloud the first question: 4 plus 7 equals…. He hopped on the number 4 and as he walked he counted, 1, 2, 3, 4, 5, 6, 7 and then he would yell, "4 plus 7 equals 11." Then he dropped down on the floor and worked the problem in the workbook. Next question: 11 plus 17 equals…. He stepped on number 11 to begin his counting. When he finished the page he rolled up his paper and stowed it away with his math book.

Did our math line work? Within a few days of using it, the paper was crumpled but his ability in addition was cemented, as was his love of math and his appreciation of his smart, fun mama. We bought another roll of paper and he helped create his new number line. Using the same concept, except walking backwards this time, he learned the concept of subtraction. This proved even more successful. I believe it was this simple exercise which laid a firm foundation for his early success in the field of mathematics.

Debi says

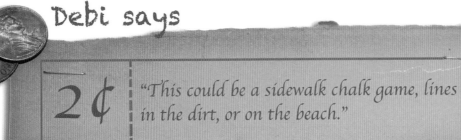

2¢   "This could be a sidewalk chalk game, lines in the dirt, or on the beach."

Dot to Dot

From the time my babies could sit in the highchair I started using flash cards with words or large dots on them. The dot cards were quite amazing. I kept cards that would only have, for instance, three large red dots on them. I would hold one up and say, "Three; three red dots." I did this with up to 15 dots. The brain appears to recognize the numbers easier at a young age. I never said, "How many?" I only told them how many. I did the same with word cards. I might only show them three cards each morning, and then only a flash of that card, yet it worked. The box that contained our dot and word cards stayed under the highchair ready to be used as each one of 9 children began to use the highchair. Of course, all the children watched the baby learn their flash words and dots, so it reinforced the learning for them. By the time each child was four, he/she could read and count, besides add and subtract. With 9 children to homeschool, any head start was a winner. My policy was and still is: *Any truly good idea is always easy to implement.*

Counting Bucks

For teaching multiplication, I used pennies Grandma saved for us. From 2 years old to 10 years old the children learned. The first day, we started with 10 pennies. Each day we added a new stack of 10 pennies until we had a heavy box of pennies being stacked and counted. As the stacks grew, we put them on colored paper to separate the groups. Leftover change or partial stacks of pennies was the next step in our math lessons. After two or three weeks, counting pennies had lost its thrill, so I told the kids it was time to add it all up so we would know how much we had to spend, and then we could all go out to eat. The math lesson was super-charged as the money was carefully counted and recounted, and then the older children figured out how many dollars and change it would be. On paper the children divided up the money in respect to how much each child would eat.

That is when I pulled out the paper bank rolls to stuff our pennies into. While we stuffed, I talked about what I had learned off the internet about how pennies, nickels, and dimes are manufactured. This opened up a whole new area of thought. The kids wanted to know why the government didn't just make new money and give everyone all they needed. Now I had some thinkers! We had lively discussions for weeks due to this project.

The whole gang went to the bank to exchange the pennies for cash. Everyone in the bank was aware that these math pennies were soon to be lunch. When we sat down to eat our burgers and fries, it was the most memorable lunch ever. With a little nudging the kids remembered the money we had saved for the tip. They looked at the waitress with new respect as we left all the rest of the money on the table. We only did this once, yet my grown children all reflect back to that penny count as a key time in their lives.

The boys counting Daddy's change

2 ¢

"*Most children never learn to question or think because information is fed to them. Information is soon forgotten, but a mind that learns to question will grow.*"

Grandfather's Gift of Change

Even though I am only 15 years old, I want to tell you how my grandfather communicated to me the idea of spending money wisely.

I was just 12 years old when he brought me to the grocery store and handed me the grocery list with money to pay for it. He told me that I had to get everything on the list with the money in hand, but whatever was left over I could keep. Looking at those twenty dollar bills was so exciting until I started down the aisle of the store with my calculator, adding up each item. Several times I had to go back and find a lower-priced item. I finally finished my list, and I carefully went back over it to make sure I had everything. As I unloaded my cart, I was very happy to know that I had some money to spare—just some change—but I had managed to buy everything. Today, three years later, I can't remember how much change was left from that first shopping expedition, but I do know that what I learned was priceless. So, here is a big thank you to my Papa. Love, Anne.

Refrigerator Math

I use a dry-erase marker in teaching, and just by accident I learned that a refrigerator and the washer and dryer can be used as a whiteboard. It is handy for "kitchen school."

City Slicker Math Class

Some days it is just too nice to stay inside and do school so we head to the sidewalk. I have a big pail of large, easy-to-wash-off, colored chalk which we use to write down our math questions. We do hopscotch math by drawing the lines and jumping as I call out the numbers to add, subtract, or multiply, depending on the level for each child. Sometimes we use shaving cream instead of chalk. Late in the afternoon, the school children walk down the sidewalk and marvel at our creations. By evening, we wash it all away and start again.

Measuring Tape

I keep a measuring tape fastened to the refrigerator and some dry-erase markers on top. For snack time, I give oranges or apples. One child measures each one, and with the marker I write the size on our refrigerator under the word "circumference." If we have pie, a circle is drawn and a child divides it up with the marker before it is cut. Often fractions are added to our refrigerator for each snack time. Those one-minute lessons can really add up.

Eating the Sum

I make hard cookies using alphabet, number, and math symbol cookie cutters (from Sweet Celebrations catalog). We use these to make words, do math, and after a few days they are rewarded by getting to eat the sums.

Math Food

We bake bread once a week and the whole family gets involved. It is a time we set aside to teach measuring, sifting, designing, and baking. When we see specialty breads in the store, they want to find recipes to make that bread. We also sell some of our bread so they take pride in their accomplishments in this area.

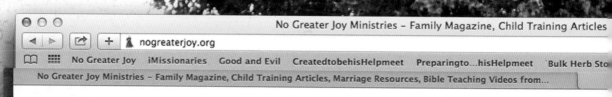

No Greater Joy Ministries – Family Magazine, Child Training Articles

nogreaterjoy.org

No Greater Joy   iMissionaries   Good and Evil   CreatedtobehisHelpmeet   Preparingto...hisHelpmeet   Bulk Herb Sto

No Greater Joy Ministries – Family Magazine, Child Training Articles, Marriage Resources, Bible Teaching Videos from...

Search   Websites and Resources   🔍

Websites and Resources for Math

- **The Math Worksheet Site**
  Here you can create an endless supply of printable math worksheets. The intuitive interface gives you the ability to easily customize each worksheet to target your student's specific needs. This way, you can add practice that your student needs to a curriculum you already like, or you can be freed from the constraints of a workbook or textbook that gives either too much or too little practice. http://themathworksheetsite.com/
- **More math worksheets and printables**
  http://www.edhelper.com/math.htm
- **Homeschool Math**
  Great website with loads of printable worksheets.
  http://www.homeschoolmath.net/
- **Math Games**
  Fun math games for computer or mobile devices.
  http://www.coolmath-games.com/
- **Khana Academy**
  Math videos that explain concepts, with interactive tests and games. This site also offers other subjects but it's not from a Christian perspective so proceed with caution in the science departments. https://www.khanacademy.org/
- **ABYCA**
  Math games that you can play, divided by age and subject.
  http://www.abcya.com/
- **Purple Math**
  Algebra lessons written with the student in mind. These lessons emphasize the practicalities rather than the technicalities, demonstrating dependable techniques, warning of likely "trick" questions, and pointing out common mistakes. The lessons are cross-referenced, and include a search box on every page. http://www.purplemath.com/quizzes.htm

- **Think Quest**
  This web site is designed by kids for kids. It examines things like stocks, bonds, and mutual funds plus teaches principles of saving and investing. It also includes a stock market game.
  http://library.thinkquest.org/3096/

- **Federal Reserve Bank of San Fransisco**
  American currency has spanned centuries of evolution and numerous transfigurations to become what we carry in our wallets today.
  http://www.frbsf.org/publications/federalreserve/annual/1995/history.html

- **Foundations in Personal Finance**
  89% of teens want to learn how to make their money grow. Yet for decades, very few schools have provided any type of money-management instruction. Dave Ramsey has created a turn-key curriculum designed to provide students with sound financial principles that will guide them into adulthood. http://www.daveramsey.com/school/foundations/

- **Stock Market Game**
  The stock market game has been used successfully to teach personal finance classes for grades 4-12. Available for a donation of at least $100.
  http://www.sifma.org/smg-at-home/index.html

- **Saxon math books**
  https://www.hewitthomeschooling.com/Materials/mSrchSubject.aspx?s=MA

- **Making math fun**
  Math is a crucial skill for kids to learn. We use it everyday from problem solving to computations. However, many parents believe that math is dry, dull, and boring. What many people (and some curriculums!) don't realize is that math can be fun!
  http://handsonhomeschooler.com/2012/05/5-days-of-making-math-fun-games.html

- **Teaching Math with Lego**s
  http://www.oneperfectdayblog.net/category/numeracy/

- **Bobby Sue's homeschool ideas Pinterest page**
  You can find lots of ideas for making math fun on my Pinterest page.
  http://www.pinterest.com/madewithtlc/debs-homeschool-book-ideas/

Pro

Shalom's Heart...
Homeschooling

Pearl Kid #4

When a child is young, the parents' training, teaching, and schooling is just a part of everyday life. At this age, children's brains are just big sponges, and whatever you put there is what they will know. You might think they are too young to understand, but they are constantly learning things by building on what they already know.

I started teaching Gracie her letters when she was a newborn. I would say, "Look Gracie, this is your name, and this is the letter A." She would just look up at me and grunt, but I knew that someday she would smile and identify the letter "A." I was laying a foundation—for me, as well as for her. In everything we do, I am teaching her. "This is a blue blanket, a yellow balloon, a green shirt." Never would I simply say, "This is a shirt," or "that is a toy." Everything has an opposite, or a contrast to something else, or a specific color, or it is long or short, or it matches this or that. Things are always described as "two toys," or "one" car and "three" trucks, and on it goes. It never seemed odd to me that my two-year-old could read her letters and know all her colors, even differentiating between colors like peach and rose. As I write this, Gracie is sitting on the floor playing with Play-Dough and talking: "This is green pie and a blue plate setting on a white floor. Look, Mama, your skirt matches my shirt. I am making a round ball, but it looks like a square instead."

Everyone laughed at me the day I went out and bought a bunch of Dollar Store school books when she was just a baby, and especially as I started going through them with her. But I just laughed right back, because I was having fun, and I was teaching my little girl how to read. She will always love to learn, because it has always been so much fun.

At work, she sits on my lap and watches me as I fill CD cases here at No Greater Joy. I count out loud, "There are one, two, three CDs in this case." It never slows me down from my work, and counting is now a normal part of her life. If I had put her down on the floor to play and not talked to her, she would not have learned anything except that Mama's hands move very fast. Following the scriptural pattern, I continually pour into her life "here a little, and there a little." Over time, it has added up to quite a lot, with virtually no extra effort.

Isaiah 28:10 "For precept must be upon precept, precept upon precept; line upon line, line upon line; here a little, and there a little…"

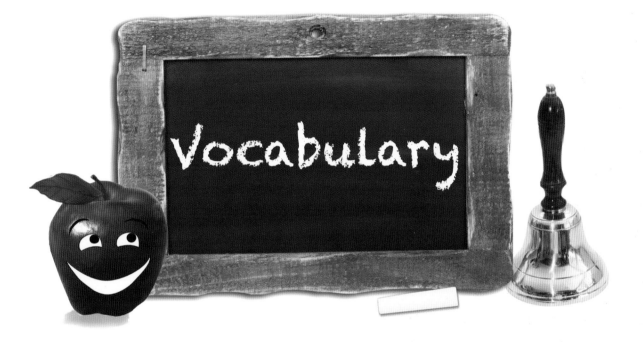

"What's **antidisestablishmentarianism** *mean?*

Send me your **BIGGEST** *word for our next*
volume of **The Big Book of Homeschooling**."

Debi

 Websites and Resources for Vocabulary found on page 56-57

Vocabulary Code

At first, my husband I were just trying to have a private conversation without the kids taking over. We would talk in code, but then the kids would rush to look up words so they could figure out what we were trying to hide from them. I would say to my husband, "We need to stop at the store to buy some bovine lactation as well as some fermented curds." After the first time, the kids knew we needed milk and yogurt so they would call out, "Get blueberry yogurt." Or I would say, "Your patriarchal ancestor called and invited us to go indulge in 'aquafying' this weekend." Dad would answer, "We will go, but only if the kids can figure out what we just said—without asking anyone." Of course the kids caught on to our meaning in a flash— we were going to Gramp's for the weekend to enjoy the lake. The kids' vocabulary grew faster than ours did, even their foreign language skills, as that was what we tried next. We tried spelling out our communications for a while, but they quickly caught on to that as well.

Byword Family

I make a new flash word each week. Over the years that has translated into a LOT of words. For the last several years, the children have selected the word. Now that my children are getting older they use the flash words as a vocabulary builder. We have become a "byword" at church. Any new or really big word, and someone will say, "Oh, that's a McMaster word." You can believe the notoriety has really, really made word masters of this family!

Drive Through

I use flash cards in the car. My oldest son, age 8, will hold up a card with a picture, word, or dots on it. Each child takes their turn calling out the answer. He, of course, puts up only pictures for the youngest child so she can participate and be successful in her answers, but she is learning by watching the other children. It keeps them focused and busy, so driving is easier, and they are learning.

Mobile Education

If you can't beat them, join them. I saw that driving was a great school time, so I started always keeping a history or science book in the car so that when we were on the road someone would have a reference to help start the question time. The children would take turns answering (with the older helping the younger); that way everyone had an opportunity to play. It made driving time pleasant and productive, and it was a great way to increase our knowledge.

A Punctuation Bible Lesson

Each day, I would quickly type in a Bible verse and print a copy for each child, always leaving out all the punctuation and an open spot for a missing word, which would be our day's spelling word. The children would open their Bibles to the proper verses, and as they read along they would correct the punctuation and fill in the missing words. This simple exercise covered the subjects of reading, writing, spelling, grammar, and Bible.

Play the Synonym Game

Any time and any place I played the synonym game. It kept my children on their toes, and when other children were present it caused a big, "What's going on?" which my children loved. For example: I would say, "This is the Synonym Game," and then call out a common noun such as the word house. The children immediately start calling out synonyms such as: dwelling, home, cabin, apartment, castle, trailer, tent, cave, etc.

Play the Homonym Game

We also played the Homonym Game. I usually started this by making a humming sound which alerted the children of the coming game. This humming sound reinforced to the small children that homonyms are words that sound the same. Then I call out a phrase, "I can see… SEE." The children respond, "The deep blue sea." Then we all hum together…SEE. The kids would try to harmonize which was really fun. It always cracked us up. It would cause the whole family to start giggling at church when the poor preacher happened to use a word that was part of our Homonym Game the previous week. Some folks think homeschoolers are weird—and sometimes it is true—but only a little.

I SEE the SEA

Homonyms sound the **same** but are spelled **different**.

hot

cold

Play the Antonym Game

The children really liked this game. Coming up with opposites has more leeway, so the results were more fun. All these games came in handy for the waiting rooms, car drives, and even when we were doing chores like washing dishes or caring for the animals. People often ask me why my children always got along with each other. It was because their minds were always in gear. Even when I was preoccupied with other things, once they had played the game the momentum was established and they could take over and make it happen.

opened

closed

Let's Play School

I love inventing ways of helping my children to learn. It's a fun challenge to teach Miriam (who is 4) learn how to read. I tried a couple different methods, but I find that they bored me almost as much as they do her. Wouldn't it be better to teach through play and adventure instead of repetitious work and boring textbooks? Would it work if I could teach school in a fun and interactive way? I decided to give it a try.

"Girls, I have a great idea—today we are going to have school! It's going to be a lot of fun!" "Yay, yay, yay!" they erupted in their cute, happy, squeals. I continued: "I was thinking that you should put on a pretty dress and brush your hair. You don't want to look sloppy for school!"

While they were getting ready, I grabbed a marker and 5 pieces of paper which I folded into big flash cards. On the front I wrote the 5 short vowels, and on the back I drew a sketch of something that began with that letter. A for Apple, I for Indian, etc. I wanted to teach them the short vowels first.

I grabbed one more sheet, and wrote some numbers that we could count together. Simple I know, but I hoped it could be fun. Miriam ran up and excitedly asked, "Mom, can we ride the bus to school?"

"Sure!" I said.

"Alright," she decides, "The couch can be the bus and you can be the driver!"

"Beep! Beep!" I said as I held on the "steering wheel." On the ride there we sang songs and laughed. "Here we are!" I announced.

From there it got more and more fun. I gave them each a turn to stand in front our little class and tell their name (first, middle, and last), their age, their favorite things to do, favorite things to eat, and what colors they liked best. They loved pretending to speak in front of a crowd. Then it was my turn to teach. Boy was it fun! I was jumping around, laughing and clapping—I had their attention and it was awesome. We were using my homemade flash cards, but they didn't care. It was fun!

So, from that day on "school" is something we all look forward to. Sometimes after our little class, Miriam and I sit down at the table and practice putting some letters together to make words. Then every day or two, I add a new letter to a flash card. Also, I'm amazed at how Esther (age 2) is picking up on her letters and numbers. It tickles me so much when she runs up and says, "Momma, let's play school!"

Card Hunting

I made some flash cards with words on them. On Wednesday evenings I hide them all over the house. All the children know that Thursday morning is "Seek-and-Find School." Sometimes we even invite other children over for the game. The children begin hunting as soon as chores are over. At lunch the cards are discussed and the younger children are assisted in reading their words. Then, after the meal, each child reads aloud their words and makes a sentence that includes all their words. Each person that wants a turn can add one word from their pile to the creator's sentence. I keep a chalkboard to record the sentences. We read the minutes from the last week's sentence, which are, of course, sentences. It is often quite funny.

Beka's Memories

Summer School

"How many seeds is there, Mama?" Rysha asked me as we cut off the seed heads of the fading calendula flowers and picked the drying poppy pods. The flowers in our front yard seemed to have tripled in volume this year, thanks to the seed-gathering and sowing of last year's efforts. Three little heads bobbed around me in the bright flowers, pulling or clipping the seed heads off and dropping them in my plastic bag. "Okay, kiddoes, let's wait for a few more days for the rest of them— they're still a bit green."

Joe Courage lined the floor of our minivan with paper, and we spread out the seeds we'd picked. Here, they would have 24 hours to completely dry. I held up one little calendula seed cluster.

"Look, Rysha—here's where the petals came out all around... and then the petals got old and blew away. Now all that's left is a ring of seeds around the middle. Look how many seeds there are in one flower! Let's count them."

We counted the seeds, removing them one at a time while all three kids pressed close to watch and count aloud. "Thirty-two seeds in one flower! That means this one flower has the potential to make thirty-two more flower plants next year!"

We picked up a poppy pod shaped like a small green bean. It was dry and papery. "Watch this. When I blow on it like the wind... pop! It splits open and the seeds jump out!" The kids squealed in delight and blew on their own poppy pods.

We spread the seeds to dry more thoroughly, and in a few days we'll scatter them over the front yard for next year's summer school and blossom festival.

Phonics

Listen to the Sound

"Training the ear to hear and distinguish sounds will carry over into many areas of life."

Debi

Websites and Resources for Phonics found on page 40-41

10-Minute Word Scramble
by Erin Harrison

This is a great phonetic reinforment technique that I learned from my mother in law who is a reading specialist. I have my child write a short sentence on a strip of paper. I usually ask him to write about something he is interested in. When he does not know the next letter, I will ask him to say the word again very slowly. The letter that he initially missed was caught the second time. After the sentence is written, he uses his scissors to cut each letter out. The fun part is when I unleash my boy to scramble up all the pieces. He then has to put the sentence back together, letter by letter. This exercise can be done in ten minutes or less and he is learning great phonics and sentence structure.

2¢ | "The babies or small children you read about are now adults."

Your Pile, My Pile by Erin Harrison

To get extra practice in sight words, I would play a game with my son who struggled in learning to read. I knew it did not come easy for him, so I always tried to find fun games we could play to make him try harder without telling him to try harder. I would make flash cards with the words I was teaching him. Any time my son would read the card correctly, I would put that card in "his pile." When he was unable to read a card, it went in "my pile." I would say the correct word as I placed it into my pile so he could try it again the next round. The winner was the one who had the most in "their pile." It got to where he made sure he won every time and the results were that he could read his sight words with ease.

I've watched many unmotivated students become dynamic learners when their interests were challenged and encouraged.

2¢ "Old magazines are often available for free in the storage room at the library."

Trampoline

My little guys need action. I made large ABC cards with a number given to each letter of the alphabet: Aa-1, Bb-2, Cc-3, etc. I lay these cards around the perimeter of the trampoline and have the children run around the outside until I blow the whistle. They grab the card closest to them and that tells them how many jumps they must do before we run around again. The lowest number child jumps first. So I gather up the cards, they count their jumps, and then we lay down the cards and go again. It's fun, gives them great exercise, and keeps them learning.

Book

I have my little ones make alphabet books. I draw the uppercase and lowercase letter on a page and have them decorate it. Then I give them old magazines to cut out pictures of animals or things that start with the letter, and they glue that to the page. We even include pictures of siblings who have a name that starts with the letter. Each page is covered and then put in a binder.

Fridge ABCs

My baby is already learning. I am not waiting for her to get old enough to talk or to begin schooling. I keep a small bucket of magnetic letters close to the fridge. When I am near the fridge I pick up a letter and sing to my daughter, "I'm picking up the red number 3, the red number 3, the red number 3. Can you find a red number 3?" The first two times I helped her, but she quickly understood. She picks up a red number 3 and puts it on the fridge. She loves it.

2¢

"Small beginnings make big wins. If you skip brain training at this early stage in your child's life, it takes twice the effort to reach just half the results."

Shout it Out
Learning from Special Needs

My son is special needs. While researching and working with professionals concerning his learning issues, I discovered a totally unexpected benefit that has application to all my other children. They all learn best AWAY from the school desk. For example: While working as a group, stacking firewood, we do memorization (multiplication, poetry, Bible verses, etc.) by shouting out in rhyme what we are learning. The four-year-old learns as fast as the 9-year-old when we do this, and my special needs son is a part of the group. We often turn on exercise music and do "Shout Out School" while we are exercising. After 20 minutes of this everyone is ready to work quietly with soft classical music playing in the background. Housecleaning moves quickly and without argument now that we incorporate "Shout Out School."

39

Search   Websites and Resources   🔍

Websites and Resources for Phonics

- **Phonics Learning Game**
  Is your child learning the alphabet and each letter's sounds? Our online phonics game is a perfect companion to this learning. With three different modes, this game will aid in phonics learning at a variety of levels. From learning to testing this online phonics game is a great way for kids to learn.
  http://www.fisher-price.com/en_US/GamesAndActivities/onlinegames/PhonicsLearningGame.html

- **Letter Sounds**
  Help children make the first, vital connection between the letters of the alphabet and the sounds they represent. Children drag pictures to the letters that make the first sounds of the word that describes the picture. Voice is used to be sure that children know the right word and to reinforce the connection between the first letter and the first sound in the word.
  http://yourchildlearns.com/lettersounds.htm

- **The School House**
  Learn the art of teaching basic reading skills. Hands-on phonics lessons presented in progressive order.
  http://www.theschoolhouse.us/about.html

- **Fun Fonix**
  Phonics worksheets for kindergarten, first grade, and second grade teachers. Free printable worksheets, phonics workbooks, and online phonics games.
  http://www.funfonix.com/

- **Progressive Phonics**
  Progressive Phonics is an all-in-one reading program that is easy, fun, and totally FREE! With Progressive Phonics, ANYONE can teach a child to read and write in just a few minutes a day, which makes it ideal for parents, teachers, tutors, volunteers, and homeschoolers.
  http://www.progressivephonics.com/

- **Phonics by The Book**
  A phonics and sight word curriculum based on God's Word. It begins at the end of K level and progresses, introducing new phonics skills and sight words. The stories start in the book of Genesis (with Creation) and will continue throughout the entire Bible.
  http://thisreadingmama.com/free-reading-curriculum/phonics-by-the-book-beginning-reader-curriculum/

- **Soft Schools**
  Free phonics games, worksheets and flashcards.
  http://www.softschools.com/language_arts/phonics/

- **Star Fall**
  A free public service to teach children to read with phonics. This systematic approach, in conjunction with phonemic awareness practice, is perfect for preschool and the elementary grades.
  http://www.starfall.com/

Pearl Kid #1

The Love of Words

What is creativity in a practical sense? Making up your own pattern for a dress instead of buying one. Making up your own ABC song. Taking a six-digit number and scrambling it into a brand new number as fast as you can in your head. Making up a rhyme or a song, writing a story, coming up with a brand new recipe, asking questions about anything you can think of and finding the answer any way you can.

When I was eight years old, I really fell in love with reading. I read everything I could get my hands on and devoured the best of three libraries. One day, Mom asked me casually why I didn't write my own book. I was stunned. How had the idea escaped me? I was eight years old and had read a thousand books and still hadn't thought of writing my own. I went straight to work. For a while, I pumped out about two "books" a month. Now I'm down to one every four years. But I'm still writing. Creativity was inside of me, just waiting to be called forth.

Reading/Writing

"*Wisdom is the principal thing; therefore get wisdom:*
and with all thy getting get understanding."

Proverbs 4:7

 Amazing Biographies for Reading Encouragement found on pages 58-59

Bobbie Sue's Book List on pages 60-61

Websites and Resources for Reading and Writing found on pages 56-57

Writer's Bent
The Adventures of Jerry, Danny, and Sara

My kids love bedtime stories. Using their middle names as characters, I tell about the adventures of Jerry, Danny, and Sara. I make up stories or tell adventures from my own youth. In my stories I have the boys doing things to exemplify Christian character, such as helping others and exhorting each other to do the right thing when pressed by others to do wrong. Before there was *Yell and Tell* (a book series on training your children to resist sexual predators), I created my own version using stories I made up. For example: I had my Sara character offered money if she would just pull her panties down, but she yelled very loudly and told on the bad boys. These bedtime stories became our "Fire Drill" in possible things that could happen, conditioning my children on how to respond. My children loved, loved, loved them—they would rather have a story any day than watch a movie or go out or anything! In our stories they have been camping, fishing, hiking, biking, swimming, etc. We have even visited Mike and Debi Pearl in Cane Creek…in story!

After several months of me doing the storytelling, one of my sons volunteered to tell a story. Away he went. I learned so much about what the boys think, hope, and fear. I also learned what they value. Soon the boys wanted to record their stories, adding their homemade sound effects. They worked at learning how to type so they could transcribe their recordings. I could have used the computer program that does it, but it seemed a good thing to let them work at it. Soon they were working on a book together as a team.

The silly, boyish squabbles became history as they struggled to create that perfect audio and then video story. School soon became an outreach of their new business. Other kids, and then other parents, hired them to video birthdays and even tell tales at parties for entertainment, working in the names of the children who were there. They named their first business "Stonemen's Productions."

Vision This is more important than just an idea. This mom inadvertently gave her family a dream or a vision. Her stories that went viral became entertainment, school, and a dream that carried their family to places they never thought they could go. It all started with bedtime stories giving them a new idea of who they were in Mom's eyes and what they could do.

Great Expectations
Debi tells a story.

When our grandson Jeremiah was 5 years old, he asked his mama (Shoshanna) to tell him a bedtime story. He wanted one about huge spiders and a strong boy who could kill them. Stretching her imagination to what she thought would thrill her little man, she started a story about this little boy who was strong, true, and willing to take care of his little sister even if he was scared. Every night, he would interrupt the story with his own "take," until soon he was coming up with most of the tale. This "play pretend" nighttime tale proved more than *just* entertaining; it was an opportunity for Jeremiah to slay the scary things in his young mind and become the defender. His writing skills were doubtlessly significantly developed in that exercise as well. Days and then weeks passed, with the nighttime story growing, twisting, and turning until even Shoshanna was fascinated with the story line.

On Jeremiah's 6th birthday, his mama made him a cake with all the different "things" he had slain. It was so big it had to be put on a piece of plywood. The cake was pieced together to form a pond (blue Jell-O), forest, and a mountain (piled cake with poured icing) where all the plastic creatures roamed. That night she gave the story a "The End." He was ready to move on.

Get the NEWS

The year we moved far away from both sets of parents, we started THE NEWSPAPER. Each Monday evening, the children took pen in hand and recapped their week's adventures. This usually included the stories like the scraped knee, the visit of the strange animal that turned out to be the neighbor's dog, and the new family at church. A picture was required for each story, either hand drawn or a photo. These days I don't do much because one of the older siblings always helps the little ones write their stories. All this is scanned into the computer, then titled by our own "Boy Wonder" (4th kid down out of 9) and emailed to both sets of grandparents. Afterward, THE NEWSPAPER is printed off and carefully stashed in the family NEWSPAPER yearbook. It is amazing how often we refer back to the yearbooks to find out when a certain thing happened. During the long, dreary days of much snow, the old copies of THE NEWSPAPER are a major source of entertainment as the younger kids discover what the older siblings did when they were young. The grandparents have eagerly looked forward to each edition of THE NEWSPAPER as they watched the children grow up from afar. It has kept us connected better than the phone, or even visits, and it has been the greatest learning tool I have ever found.

Props

I use props to teach my children, and it keeps them fascinated. For instance, instead of just reading a book to my children, I try to use props. When I read Goldilocks, I use a doll, 3 stuffed bears, 3 cups, 3 glasses, and 3 chairs—small, medium, and large. As I read the story, I hold up one bear and ask, "What size?" The children reply, "Small." The same with the cup, glass, etc. It is a perfect time to also teach safety/moral lessons. I have found my children will relate back to Goldilocks being foolish when they are faced with safety, like when playing in the park.

When I told the story of Creation, I simply filled 7 bags with teaching items. Bag 1 had a light bulb, bag 2 had a jar of water, bag 3 was full of cotton, bag 4 had dried sticks, and so on. The children can't wait to see what is in the bag, and the props cause them to remember. This type of teaching is great for church school, too.

School Year Book

We always make a yearbook, basically following the style of public school yearbooks. We take pictures of all our outings, special science projects, and have short explanations for each. We document any sports or other events that set that year apart. At the end of the year, we sit together at the computer with all the pictures and put it together. We have several copies made, one for each set of grandparents, with the understanding that their copy goes to a certain child when they graduate. My oldest daughter did finish school, is married, has two young children, and is planning on homeschooling. My mother gave my daughter the stack of homeschool yearbooks she had been "holding" for her. My grandchildren LOVE them, and someday soon will be old enough to start their own yearbooks.

Putting Up Books

We have gone to the public library at least once a week for about 18 years (a LONG time!), volunteering for about an hour on most of our visits. The best thing to do when volunteering is to put away the non-fiction books. You will end up finding many fascinating books on a wide array of subjects. Modern, non-fiction, children's books have the most amazing photos!

Reading Aloud

We volunteer at our library to do "reading hour" for the small children once a week. At first it was me who did all the reading, but soon my teens took over the chore. The community children have grown up hearing us read to them, which makes them open to our ministry of gospel tracts.

Research

We really use the library! I give each of my older children a research card before I drop them off at the library every Monday afternoon. They spend several hours looking for books on the given subject so they can prepare to give an oral report on Friday evening. They also do regular weekly cleaning and organizing chores for the library in return for the joy of using library resources. All the librarians are glad to see them each week.

2¢ | *"This is the BEST homeschool idea I have seen yet."*

Reading Miracles

I never taught my children how to read…they just knew. This is how my miracle happens.

I carefully select very simple books that my toddlers will enjoy. I set up the recording equipment and then have my 7 and 9-year-old children read the books very slowly and call their younger brother and sister by name, "Hey Johnny, do you want to read this book with me? Look at this alligator on the first page. Now, read along with me. Turn to the next page that has the tiger on it. Do you see the tiger?" The book is read and then the older brother signs off, "That is such a good book. Let's read it again tomorrow; but first, let's read the book about Moses. Get the Moses book ready. I'll sing you the number song while you open the book about Moses." We try to make a new recording each time we buy new books so there is variety. Sometimes I read a book on recorder, or Dad might read one. The little ones enjoy hearing from all of us.

Every day, one of the older children gets everything ready and sits the little ones down in the recliner for their story time. It is the quietest time of the morning. Occasionally, one of us will stand behind the chair and point to where they are in the books, but mostly they are on their own.

Nap time always starts with listening to a book read from the recorder. It settles them down, and habits help keep the children focused.

All my children learned to read following along with the recorder. For the first child, I recorded the books and had her listen while I napped with the baby. By the time she was 4 years old, she was following along with the words without any effort. I could see the idea was a winner.

The children learned their sounds, colors, counting their numbers, and anything the books happened to teach, such as naming animals, places, and things. They all breezed through first grade because they already knew it all. There was so much they were already familiar with that it was mostly just doing the copy work. Originally, I got this idea from Debi Pearl's *My Favorite Homeschooling Ideas* CD. This is the BEST homeschooling idea I know.

In Pursuit of Knowledge
The Knowledge Book

I type up a bunch of questions and tape the page to the fridge. Questions such as: How many stomachs does a cow have? What causes lightning? What are the 10 Commandments? Who was John Henry? Who was the 36th President? It is like an ongoing game.

Each night at dinner, the kids can answer any question that they have learned, but it needs to be put into writing so we can store the question and answer in our Family Knowledge book. Usually our kids team up. Our daughter likes to do the fancy copy work and the boys like to research the answers. We discuss the answers at the table, which gets Daddy involved, as he always has some weird twist to offer. When all the questions are answered, we have a Family Fun Night where we usually invite special guests (children's friends or even grandparents) and then we put the questions to them. It is always a hoot.

We let the children come up with ideas for Family Fun Night. We keep a list on hand so we have several alternatives, depending on the weather and expenses. One of the favorite things to do on family nights is building a fire out back and roasting hot dogs and telling scary stories.

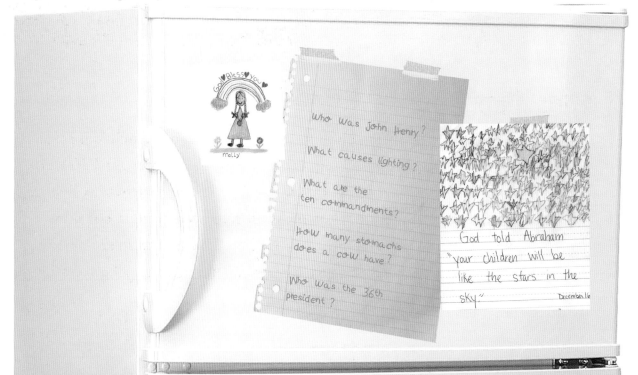

Little House

    One of the things that worked well for homeschooling our family was reading aloud time. It started when they were very young. Our first series was *Little House on the Prairie*. My husband came home early one day and sat in on our session. He started looking forward to each reading. It became the most requested event in our home. Evenings and school time were spent together learning about the pioneer ways. My family would listen for hours until my voice wore out. Although they all can read now, we still treasure our reading time together.

nogreaterjoy.org

Search   Websites and Resources

Websites and Resources for
Spelling/Grammar, Writing/Reading & Vocabulary

- **Spelling it Right**
  Learn how to spell confidently. Free printable worksheets, help, and advice from an experienced English teacher. http://www.spelling.hemscott.net/
- **Spelling City**
  This website teaches spelling in a fun way. http://www.spellingcity.com/
- **ABCYA**
  Great site for reading, spelling, and math games. http://www.abcya.com/
- **Edhelper**
  This site has printables for spelling, vocabulary, reading and comprehension. http://www.edhelper.com/
- **Online grammar and writing handbooks**
  http://www.sfreading.com/resources/ghb.html
- **Website directory**
  This site has links to grammar, reading and spelling resources. http://www.homeschoolchristian.com/curricula/langarts/index.php
- **Pathway Readers**
  Covers preschool through eigth grade. For many years educators and Christian schools have utilized these stories, poems, and reading selections to encourage Godly character and moral values. http://www.pathwayreaders.com/pathway1.htm
- **Reading Bear**
  Teaches over 1,200 vocabulary items. 50 presentations that are great for kids. http://www.readingbear.org/
- **Excellence in Writing**
  Heralded as "the best" course out there to teach your children how to write. One lady says she learned more from this course than she did while in college

working on her English Education Degree. http://iew.com
Struggling with understanding the program, and scared by the high cost?
Then check out this blog post.
http://www.visionarywomanhood.com/demystifying-institute-excellence-writing/

- **ABCteach**
  Offers a large selection of printable items including writing skills, a variety
  of forms, and writing prompts. They also have a selection of report forms
  that are kid-friendly and inspire creativity. They do follow the Common
  Core standards so use with caution. http://www.abcteach.com/

- **Daily Grammar**
  A fun and convenient way to learn grammar. By simplifying complex
  grammar subjects, Daily Grammar is a great teaching tool for anyone
  needing to refresh English grammar skills. By practicing language rules, any
  person able to read will be able to master English grammar.
  http://www.dailygrammar.com/

- **Phonemic awareness and worksheets**
  Research clearly shows the #1 reason for failure in beginning readers is the
  inability to learn all consonant and vowel sounds. These sounds (phonics)
  must be mastered in order to achieve maximum reading progress. Uniquely
  designed materials that thoroughly teach phonics and phonemic awareness.
  http://www.tampareads.com/phonics/phonicsindex.htm

- **Vocabulary**
  This is a leading vocabulary website with the best online flash-word games
  that includes word search, crossword puzzles, and Hangman.
  http://www.vocabulary.co.il/

- **Handwriting**
  A book that explains how all the letters can be made gracefully and rapidly
  using various combinations of a few basic pen strokes. It explains Spencer's
  philosophy of teaching principles which engage the mind as well as the
  hand. Teach children to write rhythmically, in concert, as the teacher
  counts. The power of this method is being rediscovered today.
  http://www.mottmedia.com/pages/publications.asp?Pub=spencer

Amazing Biographies

Suggested by Bobbie Sue

- **Alicia My Story***
  by Alicia Appleman-Jurman, WWII survivor. **14 & up.**
- **Rena's Promise***
  by Gelissen and Macadam, WWII
  Survivors. **16 & up.**
- **The Little Bear Story***
  by Richard Wheeler. **13 & up.**
- **Gianna**
  by Jessica Shaver. **16 & up.**
- **Under Fire***
  by Oliver North. **16 & up.**
- **Unbroken***
  by Laura Hillenbrand. **21 & up.**
- **Run Baby Run***
  by Nicky Cruz. **16 & up.**
- **One Bullet for Me***
  by Magdalene K. Klinksiek and
  Janet M. Hixon. **15 & up.**
- **The Hand on My Scalpel***
  by David C. Thompson M.D.
- **More Than a Slave**
  by Margaret Pagan. **12 & up.**

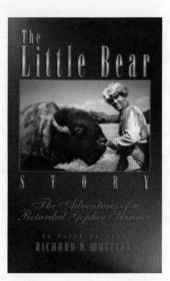

- **Lone Survivor: The Eyewitness Account of Operation Redwing and the Lost Heroes of SEAL team 10*** by Marcus Luttrell.
  If you have sons, they are sure to enjoy this book. Best if read aloud so you can edit a few words while you read.

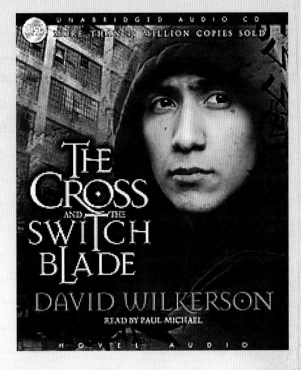

- **A Place To Hide: True Stories of Holocaust Rescues** by Jayne Pettit. **9 & up.**
- **The Cross and the Switchblade*** by David Wilkerson. **17 & up.**
- **The Story of the Trapp Family Singers*** by Maria Augusta Trapp.
- **Brother Sheffey: A Christian Who Knew the Power of Prayer*** by Willard Sanders Barbery. **16 & up.**

* means a great book to read aloud.

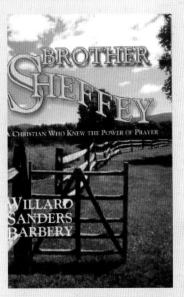

Bobbie Sue's Book List...
Fiction/Literature

- **The Day the Hurricane Happened.** by John L. Anderson. Ages 5-8.
- **Mandi Books** by Lois Gladys Leppard. Ages 8 and up.
- **Grandma's Attic** by Arleta Richardson. Ages 8 and up.
- **A Pocketful of Cricket** and **The Best Loved Doll** by Rebecca Caudill. Ages 5-8.
- **The Ox Cart Man** by Donald Hall. Ages 6 and up.
- **The Very Hungry Caterpillar** by Eric Carle. Ages 2-5.
- **Pat the Bunny** by Dorothy Kunhardt. Ages 1-3.
- **Stranger in the Woods** by Carl R. Sams II. Ages 4 and up.
- **Floss** by Kim Lewis. Ages 5-8.
- **When I Was Young in the Mountains** by Cynthia Rylant. Ages 5-8.
- **The Year of the Perfect Christmas Tree** by Gloria Houston. Ages 5-8.
- **The Boxcar Children Series** by Gertrude Chandler Warner. Ages 7-10.
- **If You Give a Mouse a Cookie** by Laura Numeroff. Ages 4-8.
- **If You Give a Moose a Muffin** by Laura Numeroff. Ages 4-8.
- **If You Give a Pig a Pancake** by Laura Numeroff. Ages 4-8.
- **A Country Mouse in the Town House** by Henrietta. Ages 2 & up.
- **A Mouse in the House** by Henrietta. Ages 2 & up.
- **Eight Cousins** by Louisa May Alcott. Ages 10 & up.
- **Little Women** by Louisa May Alcott. Ages 10 & up.
- **Little Jewel Books** by Rod & Staff. Ages 2-8.
- **The Princess and the Kiss** by Jennie Bishop. Ages 4 & up.

LAURA INGALLS WILDER

Little House on the Prairie

Performed by CHERRY JONES
Pa's Fiddle performed by PAUL WOODIEL
UNABRIDGED

- **The Squire and the Scroll** by Jennie Bishop. Ages 4 & up.
- **Little House On the Prairie** by Laura Ingalls Wilder. Ages 8 & up.
- **In His Steps** by Charles M. Sheldon.
- **Keepers At Home: A hand book for young ladies**
  by Susan Zakula. Ages 9 & up.
- **Contenders for the Faith** * by Jeffery Zakula.
- **Stories Worth Re-Reading** * by Review & Herald. Ages 6 & up.
- **Choice Stories....For Children** * by Frank McMillan. Ages 6 & up.
- **The King's Daughter: and Other Stories for Girls** *
  by J. White. Ages 6 & up.
- **Tiger and Tom: and Other Stories for Boys**
  by J. White. Ages 6 & up.
- **Derwood Inc.**
  (Peabody Adventure Series #1)
  by Jeri Massi. Ages 10 & up.
- **A Dangerous Game**
  (Peabody Adventure Series #2)
  by Jeri Massi. Ages 10 & up.
- **Treasure in the Yukon**
  (Peabody Adventure Series #3)
  by Jeri Massi. Ages 10 & up.

- **Courage By Darkness (Peabody Adventure Series #4)**
  by Jeri Massi. Ages 10 & up.
- **Llamas on the Loose (Peabody Adventure Series #5)**
  by Jeri Massi. Ages 10 & up.
- **Abandoned (Peabody Adventure Series #6)**   * means a great
  by Jeri Massi. Ages 10 & up.   book to read aloud.
- **The Bridge (Bracken Trilogy #1)**
  by Jeri Massi. Ages 9 & up.
- **Crown and Jewel (Bracken Trilogy #2)** by Jeri Massi. Ages 9 & up.
- **The Two Collars (Bracken Trilogy #3)** by Jeri Massi. Ages 9 & up.
- **Night Flight** by Gloria Repp. Ages 11 & up.
- **The Journeyman** by Elizabeth Yates. Ages 12 & up.
- **Hue & Cry** by Elizabeth Yates. Ages 12 & up.

Beka's Memories

Pearl Kid #1

My Advice to the Writer

To students, I recommend:

- Read what other people write. Read a lot of different styles: magazines, books, and articles.
- Learn to type well.
- Learn to tell a story so that both a child and an adult will enjoy listening.
- Learn to take criticism and praise with a grain of salt.
- Find out what people need to hear from you by listening to them.
- Write. Write all the time. Write without a plan; just sit down and start writing about what you see and what you think. Make the most boring subject interesting by seeing it a new way, and by describing it in detail.

Penmanship

"A person's handwriting can reveal their personality type, talents, disposition, and even their overall health. Taking time to teach your children how to shape letters can help shape the child."

Debi

Websites and Resources for Penmanship found on pages 56-57

Finger Power

While the older children do school my younger ones write in salt. I pour salt into a shallow pan and they write letters or numbers that I've placed in front of them. Some days, I fill the pan with shaving cream and they write in that.

Cards

Once a week the children send a homemade card to someone. I provide calligraphy pens and card material along with a verse carefully drawn out for them to copy. They add a flower or some other something. This has proven very helpful in handwriting skills, and it is fun.

Handwriting

My daughter didn't enjoy the handwriting exercises in her book, so I started giving her nice cards so that she could copy some of my best recipes as gifts for Grandma and other ladies. This really improved her handwriting and attitude. I also bought her a notebook and got some used magazines from the local library for her to cut out pictures. Every day she wrote a story and found pictures for her story to glue on the page. Sometimes the picture stirred up the story. Now it is her favorite pastime, and her handwriting skills have progressed to fancy calligraphy.

Bible Verses

Our daughters like to write their weekly Bible verse in calligraphy on nice cardstock. My sons like to burn their Bible verses into wood plaques. The verses are memorized and the lovely cards and plaques are saved for Christmas gifts.

Praise the Lord all ye nations: praise him all ye people. for his merciful kindness is great toward us: and the truth of the Lord endureth for ever. Praise ye the Lord.
Psalm 117

Shalom's Heart...
Learning with a Purpose

Pearl Kid #4

Every day, in a playful way, my daughter and I count numbers and read the alphabet. Just lately, I have begun trying to come up with ideas of how to keep her attention long enough to sit and practice writing and working with her hands. She is very active and has a difficult time sitting still for any time at all. I think the impatient professionals would dub her "hyperactive."

I do not want to make learning a burden to her, so I try to think of creative ways to make it delightful play. Most recently, while my husband was away on a business trip, I told Gracie, "Let's make Daddy a card." We were both excited about this idea, so for the next two hours Gracie was completely engrossed in copying and sounding out letters and drawing pictures. She was learning, but without even knowing she was learning. We both had a great time doing our "Daddy Project." More importantly, I had learned more about my child and how to keep her engaged in learning.

Most every child needs some motivation to encourage them to learn new things. The younger the child, the more immediate the reward needs to be. Telling a three-year-old that when she is twenty she will want to know how to write and read is not going to work; whereas writing a card for Daddy, who is expected home any day, was enough motivation to cause her to enjoy the challenge of learning and writing. Children are very short-term in many of their behaviors and emotions. A day is a long time. If I just told her to sit down and write letters over and over again so she will know how to read someday, she would dread the idea of school. But when we write a note to Mama Pearl, or a thank-you note to one of her little friends, she is highly motivated because there is an immediate connection to the goal that is set before her.

Yesterday, we were making a cake together when Gracie said to me, "Mom, cake starts with a K-A. Did you know that?" I laid the spoon down and said, "Let's write it with our letters." We went to the refrigerator and moved the magnetic letters around, spelling out the word CAKE. While we were there, she re-did words that we had made earlier in the week: EGG, MILK, CEREAL, DOG.

It is a great experience teaching my little girl to love to read. I look forward daily to us learning together. If I do it right, she will never dread learning, but will value it as a thrilling adventure, as do I, having been taught in the same relaxed, nonjudgmental manner.

"*A person's grammar tags them—*
it will open or close doors of opportunity."
Debi

 Websites and Resources for Spelling and Grammar found on pages 56-57

Vision

Spelling Stinks

The fact is that some folks can spell, and others can't. I can't spell, never could spell, and no matter how hard I try, I still struggle with spelling a word close enough to even use spell-check on my computer. My husband and I have written many books that have been published in as many as 45 different languages. Literally millions of people have read our writings. The sun never sets on our books. Yet neither of us can spell, although, being truthful, of the two of us he is a better speller. If we had been discouraged from writing because some teacher determined that we must spell correctly before we could go forward with writing, then I doubt if either of us would be in print today. I remember that in the first booklet we published, one word, repentance, was spelled about a dozen different ways, and every time (except the cover) was a misspelling. Since those days we have learned to use several proofers.

Many years ago, when I was a freshman in college, I was set free from the bondage of spelling. The teacher gave us back our corrected version of our first draft of a research paper that required us to introduce a controversial subject, presenting convincing arguments that would sway our readers to our point of view. I loved the challenge but was embarrassed when I saw the red ink all over the cover paper. There was so much red that it was clearly visible to everyone in the room. Then as I looked closer I saw my perfect score. I wasn't the only person that had noticed the discrepancy, as it was obvious from the murmur that there were several disturbed students in the room. The professor was a young woman, very visionary, into theater, music, and such. She walked to the front of the class and explained why some papers devoid of red ink received a failing grade and mine received a perfect score. Here, to the best of my memory, is what she said: "This is not a spelling class, nor is it a grammar exercise. It is a writing class, a place to express ideas, concepts, and reveal facts in a compelling way. I am here to teach you to express your opinion, to use the written word to reason with people. Your goal as a writer is to convince, win over, enthrall, and captivate your audience; basically to change a person's mind, will, and emotion to your perspective. This class is focused on developing in each of us the ability to touch a person's soul, and, in doing so, change them for all time."

Many children are born with the natural instinct to soar as communicators but lack the natural ability to spell. Sadly most curriculums were designed by good spellers who think all children should be forced into the proper mold as good spellers. This is why most curriculums bore the socks off visionary-type kids. I gave up socks years ago. Spelling and grammar are important mechanical skills, but good writing is an expression of the soul. Sometimes a person has an abundance of both… but usually not.

Spelling and grammar are important mechanical skills, but good writing is an expression of the soul.

Observing the natural rules of grammar does indeed enable others to understand what the writer is trying to convey. So, should you teach spelling and grammar or not? This is my professional opinion, my opinion as a grandmother of many young spellers and some not-so-good spellers, a veteran homeschool mom, and as the author of this book and many other very successful books: We should make a creative effort to instill the rules of grammar and spelling into our children to equip them to be successful in communication; but much more importantly, homeschool moms need to remember the soul of the child is more lasting than the tools of the trade. Relax, back off, and allow your child to soar. Some of you moms are homeschooling another Francis Shafer, Louis L'Amour, David Jeremiah, or Michael Pearl. Please don't squeeze the talent out of them by making them learn to spell disaster. It could be a diss-ass-stir. ~Debi

Writer's Cramp

My son hated spelling, so I put the spelling book away. Now, I pull his spelling words from his daily essays. Any word he misspells, simple or difficult, gets added to his list for the week. It is a win-win deal for him to correct his own work.

Enunciate Clearly

I make it a habit to always enunciate clearly each syllable as I talk, so my children will have better spelling skills.

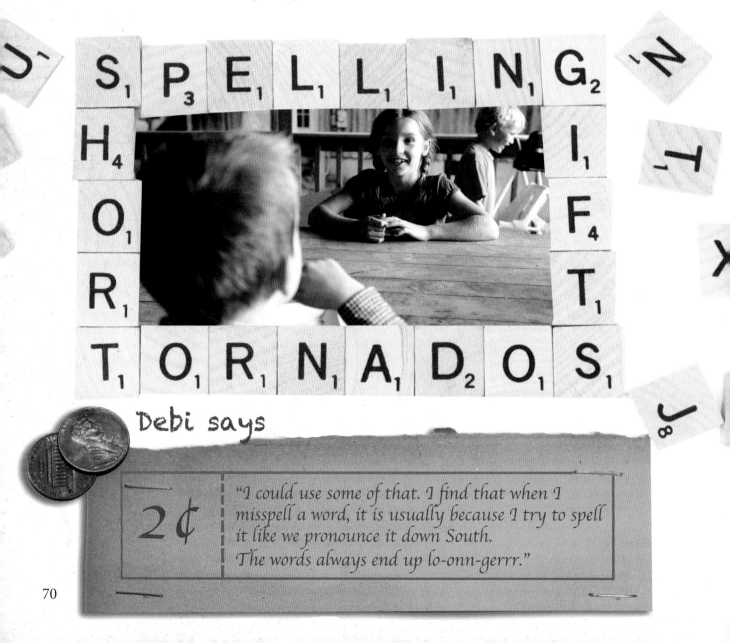

Debi says

"I could use some of that. I find that when I misspell a word, it is usually because I try to spell it like we pronounce it down South.
The words always end up lo-onn-gerrr."

Spelling Tricks:

Flash cards are very helpful to my family. Every door, appliance, piece of furniture, etc. is labeled with a card. Each day one of those words becomes the copy and spelling word. When company comes to visit, my children take great delight in amazing the other children with their knowledge of such big words. It only takes an afternoon, and after that it is always there helping me.

SPELLING FUN
Make a large cross-words game by using carboard and masking tape to make the letters.

Pearl Kid #1

Introducing Knowledge

Every night before my son goes to bed, he and his daddy go outside to look at the stars. We are twenty miles from town, and there are very few lights to dim the brilliance of the night sky.

Joe can point out the Seven Sisters (Pleiades), Mars, the Milky Way, and a few other obvious markers in the sky. He knows that God made the stars for light in the night and the sun for light during the day. This little trip outside each night takes less than three minutes, and soon Joe is being tucked into bed for prayer and a goodnight kiss.

Some folks may wonder what use there is in knowing the names of constellations and stars when you're only two years old. The obvious value is that it impresses the big people. The not-so-obvious use is the fact that when Joe goes to bed at night, he feels like he's on the inside track of knowledge. None of his friends (big or little) can point out as many constellations as he can. This assurance that he is smart has provoked Joe to question me continually throughout the day. He is consciously adding to his experience and knowledge. Sure, he's a little over-confident; but life stands ready and willing to beat the arrogance out of him in time. Meanwhile, his daddy and I are preparing him to weather that beating with a fortress of knowledge and emotional competence.

"Science begins with observation."

Debi

 Websites and Resources for Science found on pages 100-101

Planet Fan
by Erin Harrison

I was teaching my kids about the planets. I thought, why not have the kids make paper machete planets, hang them from the blades of our schoolroom ceiling fan, and watch them revolve around the sun (light bulb). Turn on the fan and watch the planets in orbit.

The Solar System

We constructed a model of the solar system out of lightweight foam and painted it with reflective material. I bought a night sky to put on the ceiling and then hung the sun, planets, and moon in place. At a yard sale, I found a clock that has a very dim, moving night sky, so when the ceiling lights are out, tiny star-shaped lights cross over our planets and the reflective ceiling adds to the whole scene. It is the coolest thing possible. When I tuck the kids in bed, I tell them my own Star Wars story about God's throne with the flashing lights and crystal floor described in Revelation. I tell about the angels being huge warriors sent to help us, and about the four beasts standing on either side of the throne saying, "Holy, Holy, Holy." They love it.

Debi says

2¢ *"This is an idea worthy of repeating. Every boy's dreams will be better, and Mom will need to become a Bible student to know how to tell God's stories."*

Experiment!

Make your own geyser using a bottle of Diet Coke and Mentos

mentos tutti frutti

2¢

"*This is the story of a REAL Grammy. Every kid needs one. Lend this book (with this page marked) to your children's Grandmother, and maybe the idea will take root.*"

The Making of a Doctor

Our 9-year-old son wants to be a doctor like his Grandpa. Grammy takes his dreams seriously. She took his picture and had it blown up full size. Every week, she sends him a learning page about a different body part and a picture of the body part to color and pin over his picture. This week, she sent him a line drawing of the brain that he colored and taped over his head. She also sent a page of how the different sections of the brain function. After reading this page, he taped it up beside the picture of his head and ran colored stings from the page to the brain. Grammy is homeschooling a future doctor…from afar.

Brain

Lungs

Make a life-sized diagram of the human body... Trace your child on a big piece of paper. Have them cut organs out of construction paper, be creative. Have the kids figure out where it all goes!

Frozen Bubbles Recipe

A simple science project that provokes lots of fun is frozen bubbles. I start by making homemade bubbles: 9 parts water, 2 parts sugar (totally dissolved), and 2 parts dishwashing detergent. Mix well but don't shake. Form the bubble maker out of metal coat hangers and blow into the cold winter air. Living in the north has its perks. This provokes all kinds of questions about the nature of the elements, and provides days of fun and interesting research. The kids then see opportunities to share their wonderful knowledge.

Exploring Bugs

We take the children to a neighboring wooded area once a month to explore. We all carry our bug bags and nets for gathering strange and interesting looking rocks, leaves, bugs, or whatever. On our way home we stop at the library to check out books that might tell us about our treasures.

The County Fair

Look up all the information you can find about your county fair. There are competitions for everything, and more and more homeschoolers are taking home the prizes! My children have entered baked goods, Lego sculptures, drawings, photography, paintings, sewing, calligraphy, and garden produce. It is work, but it is seriously accelerated learning at its finest, because *everyone* wants to win!

1st PLACE

Vision — Remember I told you that families need a vision. This is a simple, yet good vision. It might only be for one year, or it could be for several years, but it is something that will keep children or teens focused and preparing.

Shalom's "Grab the Moment"

School time is never without some new adventure in the works, and this last week was no different. We were sitting around the table working on math when my nephew, who was looking out the window daydreaming, exclaimed that it was snowing. We all ran for the door, but to our disappointment, it was not snowing but sleeting. Snow and sleet are very rare where we live, so the children were too excited to continue with school as usual—if there is a usual. The two oldest children wanted to go out and pick up the sleet, which they did. Seeing this as an opportunity to teach them something, I brought them back into the house and told them we were going to learn why it was sleeting and where it comes from. I started by putting in an earth science DVD that my sister had brought over to share with us. They had watched this before, but it had not sunk in. It was about five minutes long, and the kids were amazed at how sleet froze in midair and how hail was just tossed around before it fell to the ground. We then went to the computer where I opened the weather app and showed them how the different colors meant different things. They saw that we were in the sleeting color and that it was snowing north of us and raining south of us. We then went to the porch and looked at the thermometer to see how cold it was. We talked about the temperature and what it meant; they saw that it was above freezing right then. After this, they went outside to look at the sleet again and to bring in bowl-fulls to examine.

It has been a week since that day. I just asked them questions about how sleet and snow are made, and they have not forgotten a thing. School is fun when you look at it as an adventure in discovery and learning.

We also have a science kit where we mix different elements to make dancing water or a colorful waterfall, or just watch red cabbage water turn blue when you add baking soda, or turn pink when you add citric acid, then turn clear again if you let it sit for a few days. It raises questions that they want answered. Questions are the root of all learning.

Last week, we mixed baking soda and citric acid together to make carbon dioxide gas, and then we talked about it. Afterward, the kids watched a ten-minute science show on the lungs and how we inhale oxygen and exhale carbon dioxide. Today, as my nephew was doing school, he was reading in his second-grade science book about fish and how they take the oxygen out of the water. He stopped reading and asked, "How do they get rid of the carbon dioxide?" So we stopped working in the workbooks and went to the computer. With great excitement all five kids stood around me, and with the baby in my lap we looked it up on the computer. Soon we were learning all kinds of fun facts. The kids were interested and asked if they could make some more carbon dioxide. So back to the science kit we went. From my eight-year-old to my sister's two-year-old, we all sat around the table again and watched the baking soda and citric acid bubble and fizz. **It is when children ask questions and we take the time to answer that they learn the most.**

But some questions I am happy to leave for another day. Today, as Jeremiah was reading his book on fish out loud at the table, he read that fish lay their eggs in warm water when the days grow longer. My eight-year-old daughter, who was listening along as she did her school at the table, interrupted, "How do they make the babies? Are there daddies? Do they kiss under water?" The seven-year-old nephew excitedly jumped up and said, "Let's go look it up on the computer!"

Use every life situation to teach. For instance, when folding clothes, make triangles or squares, discuss colors, and talk about pairs.

The Wonder of Seeing Wonder Bread
(Pearl Story)

When my children were young we contacted a Wonder Bread factory and asked if we could bring the children for a homeschool tour. It was a very old factory, but it was so fascinating that I still remember it as one of the best outings ever! The fragrance of baking bread was strong even in the parking lot. The man leading us around showed us the room-sized vats where the bread was being kneaded, and then we watched as the bread was shaped and dropped into long loaf pans. We watched as the bread pans were lined up on the fast-moving conveyer belts to be moved into the open ovens, and then slowed down to bake. We saw as the fresh bread was taken out of the pans and cut into slices using thin threadlike wires. We also watched as they squeezed the cream into the middle of cupcakes. To this day, 35 years later, I never see a Hostess Cupcake or Twinkie without seeing that giant press pumping the cake full of gooey, sugary cream. It was a wonderful homeschool day-trip. Not healthy food, but a glimpse into big production. All knowledge renders us more capable and reduces the chances of us becoming victims.

Pink Palace
(Pearl Story)

Most every city has a science museum. Memphis, Tennessee has one called "The Pink Palace"—because it is pink and is, in fact, an old palace. Most science museums have special prices for schools, including homeschoolers. Sometimes there are several places working together such as the zoo, science museum, and history museum, allowing one yearly price for weekly visits to each place. It is a good investment for homeschoolers to branch out and see animals, history, science, and art. My children eagerly looked forward to our regular trips to The Pink Palace. They were significantly broadened as their imaginations were stirred and they developed curiosity in a number of disciplines and fields.

Zoology

Each year we receive a free membership to the local zoo. Regular visits can get monotonous, so I came up with side projects for each trip, such as the A-B-C Book of Animals: We took photos of 25 animals, and then with alphabet stickers and colored card paper we made a laminated book of A-B-C animals. It was a hit! We learned how to take a good photo, set up a good-looking page, and how to laminate.

The next trip we did a vertebrate study. We took 5 photos of each: mammals, fish, amphibians, birds, and reptiles. The pictures, drawings of the skeletons of each, and names and definitions of each animal were included in our Vertebrate Animal Book.

On another trip we did a hunt-and-find. We documented 10 herbivores, 10 omnivores, 10 carnivores, and 10 nocturnal animals. This required a lot of reading of the zoo signs posted with each animal. This was surprisingly fun for the gang because it was more challenging.

Day at the ZOO

Mama and Daddy helped me ride a Shetland Pony.

Galapagos Turtle
Can reach 880 pounds!
Can live up to 170 years!
That's old!

Whitetail Deer Fawn
His spots are for his protection.
It is camoflauge!

Local Universities

Local universities have free stuff! So far, we have been to the dairy barns, the observatory, the horse stables, the fisheries, and New England Astronomy Day. If any of my kids show an interest in something, say, robotics, we'll hunt down the engineering department and ask for a tour. College students are awesome with kids who show an interest in what they are studying. This also takes the mystery out of higher education.

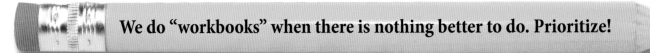

We do "workbooks" when there is nothing better to do. Prioritize!

Monarch Miracle

Find a small white egg on a milkweed stalk. Place the stalk inside a jar of water in a safe spot. The egg will hatch in a few days, and the caterpillar will eat the leaves and grow before your eyes. Keep supplying new milkweed. He'll soon search for a place to spin his cocoon. To coax him to stay where you can see him, place a large box on its side and put the jar in it with the milkweed touching the top of the box. Be sure to do it soon enough! He'll probably affix himself to the "ceiling" of the box. Within two weeks, he'll shed his skin, form a cocoon and emerge one morning as a new creation. Dip your fingers in sugar water and place him outside on a flower so his wings will dry. You and your children will want to weep and clap with joy and praise God for his beautiful creation. What a miracle!

I set a timer for 30 minutes of school and 30 minutes free. (If a child doesn't finish his prescribed work—I keep it very "doable"—during the 30 minutes of school, it spills into his free time; but that rarely every happens.) The first two 30-minute free sessions are used for chores which the children rush to finish so they will have the rest of their 30-minute sessions free.

Learning from Observation and Participation

I always had my children watch (and help) me make bread, sew, plant a garden, create an herbal tincture, or even deal with people in counseling. As I worked, everything was discussed, and afterwards, as we noted the fruits of our labor, we discussed what we could have done differently to make what we were doing easier and better. I learned with them. After watching me a short time they were given a task to help. Usually their help slowed down my progress and/or messed up what I was trying to do. BUT I stayed focused on my end-game—my ultimate goal was training my children to do and be more than I was. I wanted them to cook better, sew better, garden better, know herbs better, and deal with hurting folks better than I—and it worked—

very well. By the time my sons and daughters were 10 years old they could go into the kitchen and make a nice meal. Soon my job was to just be the chief organizer.

Observation and participation was my creed. I didn't do the observation projects found on page 90, only because I didn't think of them, but I can see they are real winners. Her ideas of observation will cause a person to develop a powerful ability to perceive the whys and wherefores of life. It is life wisdom that many people never learn. The best employee is the person that notices what needs to be done and does it. Usually that employee soon owns his own company. Observation makes that much difference in a person's life. ~Debi Pearl

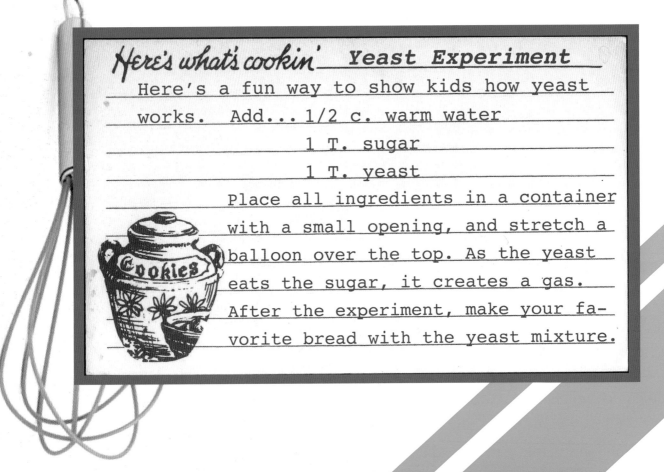

Here's what's cookin' **Yeast Experiment**

Here's a fun way to show kids how yeast works. Add... 1/2 c. warm water

1 T. sugar

1 T. yeast

Place all ingredients in a container with a small opening, and stretch a balloon over the top. As the yeast eats the sugar, it creates a gas. After the experiment, make your favorite bread with the yeast mixture.

Learning to Observe Motion and Time

Draw a picture of the western and eastern horizon as viewed from your house—west on one edge of the paper, east on the other. Make 52 copies. Once a week, plot on your picture where and at what time the sun rises and sets, making sure you note the date. Keep these in a notebook. This provides a good visual of the seasonal changes. They will be able to see the sun rise lower in the east as winter approaches, and climb back higher in the spring.

Learning to Observe Plant Growth, Weather, and Nature

Choose a plant—a tree, shrub, herb, or even a weed. A plant in a child's own garden is ideal. Draw the plant once a week all year or for the life of the plant. Make note of significant events such as weather changes, hail, rabbit attack, etc. Store in a notebook.

Learning to Observe Life

On a calendar, keep notes of things you observe in nature: First meadowlark of the season, sightings of various wildlife, etc. The children will become increasingly observant. Keep calendars and compare this year to previous ones so the children can develop an understanding of nature's cycles.

May 23rd

- Tree circumference: 5'11"
- Needles: New/tender
- Bark: Rough and dark
- Seeds: New cones forming

Michael tells a tale:
An Idea We Tabled...

Until recently, our family didn't sit down at a table, we sat down at a continent. My wife bought a perfectly clear table cloth and under it she placed several large world and national maps. We grew fond of quizzing each other on obscure countries now owned by ex-CIA operatives. My boys came to know the rivers and mountain ranges of different countries.

One day I came in to find the kids leaning over the map, all looking at the same spot, sounding as if they were competing for first place in a sports announcer's school. "There he goes across Turkey. He is now entering Iraq... No! He has turned north. He is entering Iran and making his way across to... No, he has jumped into the Persian Gulf and is entering Saudi Arabia...." They were following a bug across the world map. I thought it was a most effective homeschool method.

But last week, we came to dinner to find the geographical maps replaced with thirteen full-color posters of the human body. Now the Bible says that "no man yet despises his own flesh but cherishes it and nourishes it." I guess my wife thought there was no better place to observe the flesh than where we nourish it.

The boys quickly grew tired of observing the urinary tract during meal times. One afternoon, while eating a snack, I sat down where the boys usually sit and found I wasn't so hungry after two minutes of observing a bladder blockage. So, I moved over one seat and tried to eat a bologna sandwich while looking at a dissection of the liver. The next meal I moved around to the girls' side and studied stomach and colon cancers until I developed indigestion. I finally tried my wife's seat and studied the brain until I felt I needed a lobotomy. My position at the end of the table is graced by a ten-inch eyeball, complete with all the vessels and muscles. It reminds me of a Vietnamese dish I once ate. Did you know that the Superior Rectus muscle on the top and the Inferior Rectus muscle on the bottom enable your eye to look up and down? You didn't? Then how in the world can you read this tale?

I have studied the eyeball until I feel the whole body is an eye. But I moved to the opposite end of the table and found the answer to that verse of Scripture which asks, "If the whole body were an eye where were the hearing?" Simple. It's at the other end of the table. We are trying to find where my wife hid the world maps.

right auricle

pectinate muscles

t coronary arte

foss

lim

terminalis

ght atrium

left semilunar cusp

conus arteriosus

left auricle

ricular crest

rdiac vein

ntricular arte

entricle

chordae
tendineae

moderator
band

muscular
interventric
septum

pericardial sac

apex of heart

Debi says

2 ¢

"Hey, I think it was a great homeschooling idea.
I told the kids once they learned the various body
parts we could move on to herb posters under the
clear table cloth. They learned in record time."

tricuspid valve:
anterior cusp
septal cusp
posterior cusp

hepatic veins

inferior vena cava

anterior papillary muscle

Density Experiment
by Erin Harrison

A fun experiment I did with my kids recently was on density. We took a pint glass jar and filled it half way with water. The other half we filled with cheap vegetable oil. The oil is less dense than water, so it has to float on top of the water. This is due to the atomic structure of elements, molecules, and compounds that make it up. The kids dropped three different objects that had different masses. Before they dropped the items in, they had to hypothesize (guess) if they would sink or float. The penny had the greatest mass and it immidiately dropped to the bottom. The blue lego piece had a mass greater than oil but less than water so it stopped at the oil/water line. The leaf had the least density and so it floated on top of the oil.

Is It Love?
by Michael Pearl

In college—I think it was in physics class—the question was put to us, "If a tree fell in the forest and no one heard it, would it make a sound?" Answers flew out quickly: Of course…No…Well… We later learned that it depends on how you define sound. Do vibrations become sound as they are emitted, or must they strike an eardrum and be interpreted by the brain as sound? The question was asked, obviously, to provoke the students to consider the nature of sound. It must have been a good question, for I still remember it after fifty years. You would never hear a question like that in this Amish/Mennonite community in which we live. If they heard a tree fall in the forest, they would go out and cut it up for firewood. If they didn't hear it, they wouldn't be concerned about whether or not the squirrels heard it. They have better things to do. Nevertheless, it continues to be thought-provoking to me. Now, couched in similar terms, I will pose a question that is much more relevant. If, in the forest of humanity, someone loves, but no one ever hears them say so, is it love?

Sweet Potato Fun

This can be a fun horticulture experiment with your kids. Show them how you can start many plants from one sweet potato.

Sweet potatoes are not started from seed but by planting a sweet potato in a pot of soil. The potato will sprout and grow little shoots that will become your new plants. To start out, you can buy plants (slips) or you can buy an heirloom sweet potato or two from a farmers' market or a neighbor who grows sweet potatoes.

Do not use potatoes from the supermarket—they will likely be from hybrid plants and won't produce well. Plant the potato in a pot that is at least an inch bigger all around than the sweet potato, using good garden soil. Water well. You do not need drainage holes because the potato likes it wet.

Put in a sunny window, though it doesn't need full sun. It will do well at room temperature. When the shoots are about 2–3 inches tall, carefully twist them off at the roots, and stick them in a glass with 1–2 inches of water—this will cause them to grow roots. You can then transplant them into little pots with potting soil like normal seedlings to get them established before planting in the garden.

~ Shoshanna (Pearl) Easling

- Instead of composting the end of your celery, place it in a glass jar.
- Add water and watch a new stalk of celery grow!

Regeneration Celery!

Solar System Pancakes

Why make plain pancakes when you can make the solar system? My children keep a solar system poster board up on the kitchen wall so they can pick out which planet they are eating. Dad does the design each Saturday (Pancake Day) and they all lean over him so they can call out which planet he is pouring into the griddle.

Five-Minute Science Experts

Each week, I let my boys pick a new animal, insect, or job to learn about. Our first project was bats. During "bat week," I went to the library, got a few children's books on that subject, printed off color sheets with bats, and printed off a sheet for the letter B. I also rented some educational DVDs about bats.

We learned that bats eat bugs and fruit, so we shaped our hamburgers into spiders and ate those along with apples for lunch. We would read our bat books before bed each night and the next day we would tell Daddy all about what we learned. It took about 5 minutes every few days talking about bats for the kids to become experts on bats. I let the boys pick the subject because I knew they would love to learn about something they are already interested in.

The next week our project was sharks. I had to question myself when they boys said, "Mommy, why is that man's leg gone?" We learned how to survive during a shark attack and that sharks are actually scared to death of people!

The next week was spiders…

As the boys grew and their interests expanded, we included how to build houses, computers, shrimp ponds, and any other thing males like to know about. There are few subjects the boys can't discuss in great detail.

No Greater Joy Ministries – Family Magazine, Child Training Articl

nogreaterjoy.org

No Greater Joy   iMissionaries   Good and Evil   CreatedtobehisHelpmeet   Preparingto...hisHelpmeet   Bulk Herb S

No Greater Joy Ministries – Family Magazine, Child Training Articles, Marriage Resources, Bible Teaching Videos from...

Search   Websites and Resources

Websites and Resources for Science

- **Creation videos**
  http://thatsafacttv.com/
- **Edhelper**
  This site is not Christian so use with caution. Lots of printables and teaching tools split into categories such as food, soil, sun, metals etc.
  http://www.edhelper.com/Science.htm
- **Answers in Genesis**
  An apologetics ministry dedicated to enabling Christians to defend their faith and to proclaim the gospel of Jesus Christ.
  http://www.answersingenesis.org/get-answers/topics-alphabetical
- **It's A Young World After All**
  Online articles/book cataloging over 10 years of research by Paul D. Ackerman. Espouses the "young earth" view.
  http://www.creationism.org/ackerman/index.htm
- **Crazy Concoctions**
  Every kid has a little mad scientist hiding inside of them, and nothing is more fun than dreaming up mixtures that bubble and steam and overflow! Here are 10 crazy concoctions you can whip up at home to satisfy their need to explore and create.
  http://www.babble.com/home/8-recipes-for-disaster/?pid=19536#slideshow
- **Water Filtration**
  Build a water treatment system.
  http://www.hometrainingtools.com/water-filtration-science-project/a/1803/eid/SEN1203A/
- **Build Your Own Ecosystem**
  What happens when we introduce chlorine to our enviroment? What about other toxins? What about not adding bugs? Omit a plant? Learn how an ecosystem functions.
  http://scribbit.blogspot.com/2010/05/kids-summer-crafts-build-ecosystem.html

- **Make your own flashlight**
  A very enjoyable project for mechanically inclined children.
  http://www.instructables.com/id/Torch-made-from-coke-can-and-cereal-box/
- **Crystal Egg Geodes**
  You can find instructions on how to make them here:
  http://www.marthastewart.com/343344/crystal-egg-geodes
- **Dancing Oobleck**
  A mixture of cornstarch and water. Make cool designs with sound
  frequencies. http://www.housingaforest.com/dancing-oobleck/
- **Growing Plants**
  Grow plants with kids; do they need light? Fun experiment!
  http://herbarium.desu.edu/pfk/page11/page12/page13/page13.html
- **Chromatography**
  What color will the leaves on the trees change to this fall? Can we use
  chromatography to predict it? http://almostunschoolers.blogspot.com/
  2010/09/fall-science-part-2-leaf-chromatography.html
- **Walking Water**
  A fun project for younger kids.
  http://bncsmithson.blogspot.com/2011/08/science-experiment-walking-water.html
- **Tornado in a jar!**
  http://elliemoon.typepad.com/blog/2012/02/tornado-in-a-jar-diy.html
- **Colored water and celery experiment**
  http://tinkerlab.com/celery-experiment/
- **Walk on eggshells**
  http://www.stevespanglerscience.com/lab/experiments/walking-on-eggshells
- **Elephant Toothpaste**
  This exciting science experiment is great in a discussion on reactions, as a
  demonstration, or as an actual experiment. http://preschoolpowolpackets.
  blogspot.com/2012/01/science-experiment-elephant-toothpaste.html
- **Experiment with magic sand**
  http://www.stevespanglerscience.com/lab/experiments/magic-hydrophobic-sand

Shoshanna's Reflections

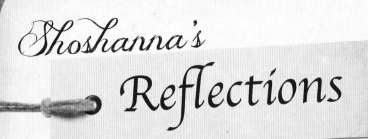

Heirloom Seeds

Heirloom seeds have been saved from generation to generation. Many people ask, "How old does an heirloom seed need to be, to be called an heirloom?" Most people agree that after a seed has been saved for over 50 years, it is an heirloom. Heirlooms are also called heritage seeds.

They can be saved 50, 100, and even thousands of years. The fruit tastes much better than hybrid or genetically modified fruits. Heirloom seeds are known to produce fruits that are more delicious, nutritious, and colorful than other types of seeds.

~Shoshanna

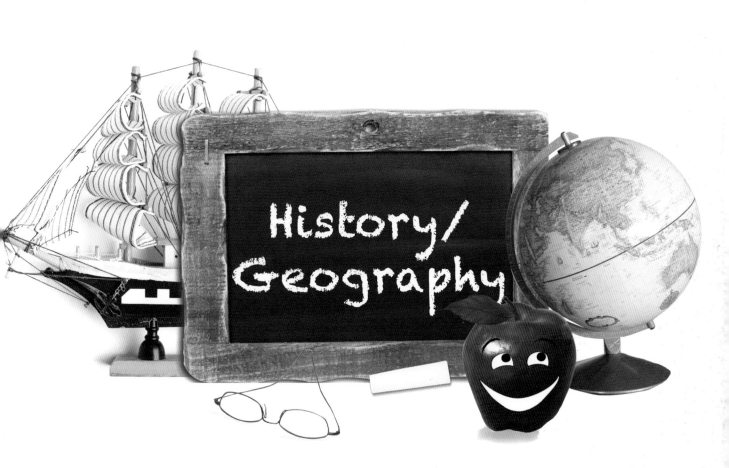

History/Geography

"Those who fail to learn from history are doomed to repeat it."

Winston Churchill

 Historical Biographies for Reading Encouragement found on pages 114-115

 Bobbie Sue's Book List on pages 116-117

Websites and Resources for History found on pages 118-119

2 ¢

"The following idea demonstrates why some children know so much. Learning can be a pain, or it can be wonderful fun!"

Playing Pretend

Once a week, I wake the children pretending to be "someone" in history. Usually the character is from something we have been reading or learning in our history books or Bible stories—although sometimes I pick a character they have never heard of so they must take the clues and look on the web to find who it is. Off and on all day long I flash back to my character. I usually try to dress a little like my pretend character, even if it is just a cap. One week, I was Louis Pasteur and talked nonstop about this terrible invisible enemy that no one believed was really there. I told stories about a bad dog biting a little boy, and how I wanted to help him but just didn't know if what I had invented would work. By the end of the day as Louis Pasteur, I knew my discovery for rabies was successful, and so did my children, because they found the library books I had checked out the Friday before and read all about him. This school year, I have been Moses, Adam, General Patton, Ronald Reagan, Martin Luther King, Fanny Crosby, and even Adolf Hitler. Through all this the kids have learned much about theater, history, music, government, war and consequences, and we have all had fun. The older children have been studying and are ready to make their debut.

Measuring Up Your Own History

Make your own measuring wall: Simply choose a wall that is clear and tall, maybe a doorway, that you don't mind getting marked up. If you think you might move, you should use a board that you can take with you throughout life. Stand your child up, bare heels against the wall, back straight, and head up. Lay a book flat on his head, pressing the edge against the wall to give you a level reference point. Mark his height with the pencil. Measure from floor to mark. Write the date, name, and measurement beside the mark—very small, because there will be a lot more marks before you are through. ~Rebekah Joy Anast

More from Rebekah (Pearl) Anast

Rebekah's Diary
Young missionary to Papua New Guinea

Available from NGJ

A-B-C Bible Verse Songs
Verses put to music

Available from NGJ

From the End of the Earth
Songs written and sung by missionary Rebekah Pearl

Available from NGJ

The Da Vinci Road: Observation and the Art of Learning

Available on Amazon.com

Key Point

Basically, anything a child learns in this environment will stick! An unwise parent might ask, "Yes, but what good is learning about bats, sharks, and spiders?" Knowledge breeds confidence; confidence won through knowledge provokes a person to crave to learn more. When a child knows fascinating information that other children or even adults don't know, it builds confidence and a desire to learn more. It is the stuff that makes high achievers. This is how to homeschool winners. Super simple…any mama can…every mama should.

The Experience of History
by Erin Harrison

When teaching my children about world history, I like to really experience it with them. First we decide what part of the world we will study EVERYTHING about. For example, when we studied about the Ancient Sumerians and the Cradle of Civilization, we went to the local library and checked out every book on the subject. We collected all our evidence to recreate that time period. I had them each write a story about a character they made up. In the story they had to investigate what the daily life was like and create a story that reflected the village life. One of my daughters wrote about a girl who was a daugher to the ruler, while my other daughter wrote about a poor village girl. My son decided to write about the battles during that time as a battle commander. I had the kids draw maps and color the maps of the Mesopotamian Valley. We read the portion in the Bible about Abraham and Sarah because they lived in the city-state of Ur. We learned Ur was in the Fertile Cresent.

After watching some YouTube videos on the subject, we were ready to take this history lesson to a new level. The kids had to pick what their trade was if they were living in an Ancient Sumerian village. I had them make an actual village outside. They built rustic looking forts and began to create things that they could trade. Each day they could not wait until History class so they could run outside and live out that time period. They made campfires to cook food on that could be traded with other villagers. We practiced the cuneiform writing on clay tablets and they could write a secret message to each other while in their village.

We ended the unit by having a royal feast. I looked up some ancient Sumerian recipes and had another homeschool mamma in the neighborhood help prepare it. I found a song on the internet from that time period using a lyre. We listened to the music, lit the candles, and enjoyed the experience of history.

Roasted Quail and Date Cookies

Ancient Spear

Unit Studies utilizing the library or web for information:

1. **Camping:** One study we did was a camping unit in which we learned all about setting up a comfortable camp, cooking, cleaning, tracking, hiking, plant/tree identifying, etc. The final test was taking a family camping trip where the children "ran" the camp. We hiked and hunted for the plants and trees that we had just learned about, hung our food from a tree, cooked over a fire, pitched our tents, etc. They learned skills that we still use to this day. Camping is so easy and fun because they happily do most all of it! Go camping!

2. **Pretending:** Pretending to be Lewis and Clark was a good unit study. We kept journals, made moccasins, created a salt water map, collected leaves, researched nature, and logged each day's journey as we followed the journals of the expedition and located the stops on the map.

3. **Bingo:** An easy rainy day project was playing Revolutionary War Bingo.

4. **Home Improvement:** The best unit studies we did were built around home improvement. You can find books and YouTube videos that teach how to paint, clean, mow, lay tile, pour concrete, or any home improvement project, and our sons loved learning and taking the responsibility to complete the work. Even my daughters got into these homeschooling projects because it meant a new room for them. Some large builder supply stores have free "how-to" Saturday workshops (such as Lowe's). We even came home with free building materials. Dad loves us taking over, as building is not his strong point.

Around the World Geography

Each afternoon for a few weeks I read aloud the book *Around the World in 80 Days* to my children. After reading a bit, we would get out the globe and see where our world traveler had gone. After that we got out a map of our city and found the road we lived on, a nearby bridge, and the closest grocery store. The next day I noticed the boys poring over the local map, marking every place they knew. They took the map with them everywhere we went for a couple weeks. Now they are very proficient map readers. It doesn't take much to open a door to a child's mind.

Beach Ball Geography

I bought a globe beach ball. The children sit on the floor and the leader rolls the ball to one child. The child has to reach down and place his finger on the spot at the top then name the land mass closest to his finger. Older children help the younger. Details progress with age.

Blindfolding Mommy

I wanted to teach my children how to give good directions. I had them follow me through the house, and as I walked, I talked. "We are walking through the front door, which faces east. The sun comes up in the east each morning and shines into the front window of our living room. The door out of the living room leads to the hall, which is about 10 feet long. The first right is the…" After explaining our goal, I gave each one a starting place and told them to write directions which will lead to the kitchen table. When they were finished, I had them put a blindfold on me and I began following their directions as they read them aloud. I ran into walls, made missteps and basically never made it to the kitchen table. The next day they tried again, with the reward going to the child who could get me to the kitchen table without any mishaps. This became an instant hit and a much discussed venture. Each week, we stretched out a little further—the yard, the neighborhood, and then the city. We bought a world map and started "traveling" everywhere, and our directions began to include ships and trains, hours and time changes, etc. It was our afternoon sport. At first, all I wanted was for the children to learn directions; however, this one activity became the turning point in our children's education in all areas of learning.

Now all my children are excellent at giving directions and have a great deal of confidence. At church the other day, a lady was trying to give directions to another lady on how to get to the upcoming school play, which required several odd turns due to construction going on in the area. My youngest child (9-year-old son) politely said, "Excuse me, Mrs. Arnold, if you turn right you will be at Hardees. The correct directions are…" Both ladies stared in total amazement and then looked at me obviously impressed, "Where does he go to school?" He quickly answered for me, "Oh, my mom homeschools us and she is really good at her job." So, we let our light shine, and the light of knowledge makes it easier to raise children who feel good about themselves.

Sticking It

I ask Daddy to teach our sons geography. The boys think Daddy is a really good teacher, and it appears they are correct, as they know more geography than anyone in church including our pastor! This is his technique: My husband put up a world map on the garage wall and bought some darts. The men of the family rush out to the garage after dinner in order to do school. They aim for certain countries or try to guess what country they hit. All their friends beg to come and do school with them. I wonder why? I voted for suction arrows…Daddy and the boys thought the other kind was better. Daddies know best.

Making History Films
by Erin Harrison

Any time we do a history unit, we like to get the video camera out and play-act history. We all dress up in costumes and bring out other props. One year, as we were studying about the beginnings of America and how the Pilgrims came from Europe on a boat searching for religous freedom, the entire neighborhood came to play. Some came dressed in Native American costumes, while the rest of us wore our Pilgrim attire.

We jumped atop my husband's flatbed trailer and pretended we were on the big ship getting seasick. All we had to eat was stale bread. When we found shore, the Native Americans greeted us.

The entire group played and learned all throughout the day. For our lunch break we talked about how the Native Americans would make cakes out of the corn they grew. It was something they taught the Pilgrims. So we made corn cakes over the open fire and it was our reinactment of the first Thanksgiving. Another homeschool girl came to film everything. The kids were having fun learning while building memories to last a lifetime. Every Thanksgiving we love to watch our film.

> **2 ¢**
>
> *"Reading Social Studies, History, and Science stories aloud to all the children as a bedtime story is fun and all the children learn together."*

History Record Book
by Erin Harrison

One of the ways I like to incorporate fun learning in History is by making a book for each unit study. For example, I made a list for the book pages when studying Ancient Egypt. For the 1st page, they had to design the cover and I told them to make it really colorful. They even used glitter and other sparkling jewels that they glued on.

- Page 2—Map of upper and lower Egypt (it was fun to stick pyramids on this)
- Page 3—Drawing of daily life of the common Egyptians
- Page 4—Drawing of the Pharaoh
- Page 5—Drawing of a story from the Bible in Egypt (Joseph/Moses)
- Page 6—Drawing of the Pyramids (including mumification and beliefs)

They had to do all the research in books and on the internet. At the end of the project, they had a basic outline to follow in writing a research paper all about Ancient Egypt. They will have a book and a research paper for each civilization around the world and in the process they are gaining an understanding of why people believe the way they do. They will know how to pray for other nations and eventually they will be able to reach them with the gospel.

Historical Biographies

Suggested by Bobbie Sue

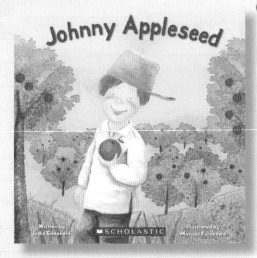

- **Johnny Appleseed**
  by Jodie Shepard. **Ages 4-8**
- **Johnny Appleseed**
  by Scholastics. Hello Reader
  Level 1. **Ages 6-10**
- **Children of the Storm:
  The Autobiography of
  Natasha Vins**
  by Natasha Vins. **Ages 13-16.**
- **Eric Liddell**
  by Catherine Swift. (Men of Faith Series) **Ages 12 & up.**
- **Florence Nightingale: The Lady of the Lamp**
  by Basil Miller. (Women of Faith Series) **Ages 12 & up.**
- **C.S. Lewis**
  by Catherine Swift. (Men of Faith Series) **Ages 12 & up.**
- **William Wilberforce: Exceptional Lay Leaders**
  by Lon Fendall. (Heroes of the Faith) **Ages 9 & up.**
- **Give me Liberty: The Christian Patriotism of
  Patrick Henry** by David Vaughan. **Ages 15 & up.**
- **Moms Who Changed the World**
  by Lindsey O'Conner.
- **Original Intent: The Courts, the Constitution
  & Religion** by David Barton.
- **John Adams** by David McCullough.

- **All the Presidents' Children** by Doug Wead.
- **Lady of Arlington: The Life of Mrs. Robert E. Lee** by John Perry.
- **Unshakable Faith** by John Perry.
- **God's Mighty Hand: Providential Occurrences in World History** by Richard Little Bear Wheeler.
- **Survivors: True Stories of Children in the Holocaust** by Allan Zullo. **Ages 12 & up.**
- **Persecution: How Liberals Are Waging War Against Christianity** by David Limabugh.
- **Lives of the Signers of the Declaration of Independence** by Benson J. Lossing.
- **Great American Statesmen and Heroes** by Catherine Millard.
- **Sergeant York and the Great War** by Tom Skeyhill.
- **Titles by Kenneth Davis:**
    - **Don't Know Much About History**
    - **Don't Know Much About the Pilgrims**
    - **Don't Know Much About the Pioneers**
    - **Don't Know Much About the 50 States**
    - **Don't Know Much About the American Presidents**

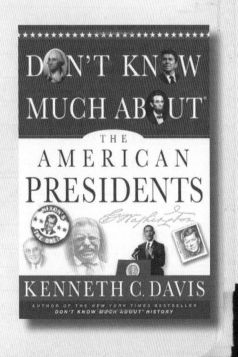

* means a great book to read aloud

Bobbie Sue's Book List...
Historical Fiction

- **In Between Two Flags** A book series by Lee Roddy. In the first book, readers join three very different young people. They were unlikely friends until crushed together in the crucible of the American Civil War. These three form an indestructible bond that plunges them into betrayal, tragedy, and overwhelming odds. On a long journey of honor and redemption, each reveals what is in their heart.
- **G.A. Henty** has many books that are great for boys. **Ages 9 & up.**
- **Everette T. Tomlinson** Many great books by this author. **Ages 9 & up.**
- **Wild Horse Winter** by Tetsuya Honda. **Ages 1 & up.**
- **When I Was Young in the Mountains** by Cynthia Rylant. **Ages 5-8.**
- **The Courage of Sarah Nobel** by Alice Dalgliesh. **Ages 7 & up.**
- **Carrie and the Crazy Quilt** and **Carrie and the Apple Pie** by Nelda Johnson. **Ages 8 & up.**
- **A light Kindled: The Story of Priscilla Mullins** by Tracy Leininger. **Ages 7 & up.**
- **Nothing Can Separate Us: The Story of Nan Harper** by Tracy Leininger. **Ages 7 & up.**
- **The Land Beyond the Setting Sun: The Story of Sacagawea** by Tracy Leininger. **Ages 7 & up.**
- **Unfading Beauty: The Story of Dolly Madison** by Tracy Leininger. **Ages 7 & up.**
- **Keep the Lights & Burning Abbie** by Peter and Connie Roop. **Ages 7 & up.**

WILD HORSE WINTER

Tetsuya Honda

- **Welcome to Kirsten's World 1854** by Susan Sinnott. **Ages 8 & up.**
- **Welcome to Josefina's World 1824** by Yvette La Pierre. **Ages 9 & up.**
- **The Story of Ruby Bridges** by Robert Coles. **Ages 8 & up.**
- **Welcome to Felicity's World 1774** by Catherine Gourley. **Ages 9 & up.**

- **Welcome to Addy's World 1864** by Susan Sinnott. **Ages 8 & up.**
- **Welcome to Samantha's World 1904** by Catherine Gourley. **Ages 8 & up.**
- **The World of John Smith** by Genevieve Foster. **Ages 10 & up.**
- **The World of Columbus and Sons** by Genevieve Foster. **Ages 10 & up.**
- **George Washington's World** by Genevieve Foster. **Ages 10 & up.**
- **Augustus Caesar's World** by Genevieve Foster. **Ages 10 & up.**
- **Abraham Lincoln's World** by Genevieve Foster. **Ages 10 & up.**
- **Escape From Warsaw*** by Ian Serraillier. **Ages 12 & up.**
- **Jonny Tremain** by Esther Hoskins Forbes. **Ages 9 & up.**
- **In Search of Honor** by Donnalynn Hess. **Ages 12 & up.**

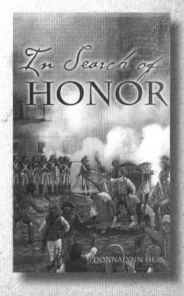

*means a great book to read aloud.

nogreaterjoy.org

Search | Websites and Resources

Websites and Resources for History

- **U.S. Presidents**
  Fun site to browse and learn about U.S. presidents.
  http://www.mistergworld.com/12-002.htm
- **Constitution Classes**
  Great for the whole family. Free constitution classes from Hillsdale
  College. https://online.hillsdale.edu/register
- **History Worksheets**
  http://www.edhelper.com/United_States.htm
- **Beautiful Feet**
  An approach to history through literature. http://bfbooks.com/
- **American Journeys**
  Over 18,000 pages of eyewitness accounts of North American
  exploration, from the sagas of Vikings in Canada to the diaries
  of mountain men in the Rockies. Read the words of explorers,
  Indians, missionaries, traders, and settlers as they lived through
  the founding moments of American history.
  http://www.americanjourneys.org/index.asp
- **My Father's World**
  A comprehensive four-year curriculum that integrates Bible,
  history, and English (3 full-year credits). Each year has detailed
  daily lesson plans and a complete book package.
  http://www.mfwbooks.com/category/M50/50

- **State History**
  Learn state history from a Christian perspective.
  http://www.statehistory.net/

- **Roadmap to America**
  A complete history curriculum for a new century of American youth. Textbooks by former secretary of Education William J. Bennett.
  http://www.roadmaptolastbesthope.com/

- **United States Bingo Game.**
  http://deceptivelyeducational.blogspot.com/2011/09/united-states-bingo-game.html

- **Board Games Geek**
  Take an old Guess Who game that is missing pictures and turn it into a president's game! You can play it the same way, but add questions like who was the 16th president, did they have five kids, etc… great way to make the history of American presidents stick!
  http://boardgamegeek.com/image/463690/guess-who

- **Between Two Flags**
  More information available on page 116.
  http://www.leeroddybooks.com/

Shoshanna's
Reflections

Pearl Kid #5

Mirror of our Reflection

From the time Jeremiah was a baby, the moment he wakes I cheerfully say, "Good morning, sweetheart!" He always smiles back in delight, and I go on to talk to him about the wonderful day ahead. This sets the tone for the day, and every day is a good day. Happy, confident, aggressive, as a toddler and then a small child, he knew his mama loved him. He has grown up so much. Now he is five and I say to him, "Do you know you are the best kid ever?" "Yes!" he says. "I know, Mama. Do you know you are the best Mama ever?" We laugh and hug. I have found I am raising my reflection. Now Penelope Jane has joined our play. She is eight months old and delights in her brother as he does in her. I see my son starting his sister's day off with a smile as he talks with her and delights in her.

My children reflect everything I do: The way I greet and talk to Daddy, the way I treat others, and the way I live life. Everything I do, everything I say—they look at me and learn. By the time a child is five years old, his brain is 90 percent developed—and his soul is 90 percent developed as well. The heart is well on its way to learning empathy, love, kindness, goodness, gentleness, courage, strength, and steadfastness—or else anger, laziness, pouting, envy, greed, and lust.

I look around and I see parents everywhere raising their reflections. Each child is unique, but still reflects who is raising him. I look at myself and I ask, am I what I want my kids to be? "More is caught than taught," my daddy always says. Your children are your reflection. Look at your reflection and smile. It is a two-way mirror.

~Shoshanna

"*Learning a foreign language opens the brain and doors of opportunity.*"
Debi

 **Websites and Resources for Foreign Language** found on pages 130-131

2¢ | *"We don't pour our lives into our children to keep them."*

Language Learning

What's for lunch? Spanish! I use a dry-erase marker to write the day's meal plan on the refrigerator. I write it in Spanish. The older children use the Spanish dictionary to look up what we are having and how to pronounce it. We listen to songs in Spanish and sing them before we eat.

Para Comer...
Tacos duros con
    carne deshebrada
ensalada
limonada Fresca

Beginning With Words

Beka's Memories...

For weeks now, my two-year-old has had the obnoxious habit of repeating himself over and over. At first I continued to answer him patiently—the same answer ten times in a row.

Next I resorted to ignoring him; but the questioning went on. Finally, I threatened to spank him if he kept asking the same question after he had received the answer. Then one day, he asked me a question that did not need an answer—and then asked it again in a different way. "I see no stars up there, Mom?" "Mom, do I see no stars up there?"

A light went on in my brain. I began to recall my own experiences with language learning in Papua New Guinea. Could my two-year-old possibly be cognizant enough to be learning his first language in such a structured manner? So, for the first time, instead of answering his question, "I don't know whether you see any stars or not, Joe," I repeated his phrase back to him with the proper grammar. "I don't see any stars up there, Mom." He looked at me with absolute delight and jumped up and down yelling, "I don't see any stars up there, Mom!" The next few days were an intense learning session. Joseph's ability to talk grew by leaps and bounds. He questioned me continually; and now, instead of answering what had appeared as dumb questions, I would carefully articulate the grammar and phonetics of a whole exchange for him. He repeated me until he could say it all properly without coaching. Joe: "You got to wash a dishes, Mom?" Mom: "Do you need to wash the dishes, Mom?" Joe: "Do you need to wash the dishes, Mom?" Mom: "Yes, Joseph, I need to wash the dishes. Would you like to help me?" Joe: "Like to help me?" Mom: "I want to help you, Mom." Joe: "I want to help you, Mom." His affection for me became hilariously dear. We were close before, but now we had become best buddies in just a few hours. I was suddenly the only person in the world who could tell him exactly what he wanted to know.

My curiosity was aroused; did all toddlers face this problem? I began to listen in Wal-Mart and the bank when I went to town. What I heard was different levels of understanding. Some children seemed to be under the impression that there wasn't necessarily a correct way to speak, perhaps because the adults in their lives simply

Beka washing clothes

repeat their baby-talk back to them, thinking it cute. Other children had obviously discovered the truth and were in various stages of learning with their oblivious teachers. I can sympathize with these kids in their efforts to learn a language from a clueless adult.

I spent two years among the Kumboi people of Papua New Guinea. Most of that time was spent on linguistics and translation. I squatted for hours in the smoke-filled cookhouse in the center of our village, practicing the words I learned and trying to pick up new ones. The villagers loved to hear me talk. It amused them to hear a grown person falter and slur words just like their toddlers. I encountered the same problem Joseph often does when my Kumboi friends failed to repeat the words I said correctly. Their first response was to say them the same poor way I had because it was funny.

Among my friends was a young married girl from one of the most remote and uncivilized villages in the region. She was often teased for forgetting to wear a shirt or comb the debris out of her hair in the morning. Natalin did not speak the trade language at all when I first came and was confined to the local tribal language alone. Natalin was my favorite language helper above all. She was a natural teacher. When I said a word incorrectly, Natalin did not think it was funny; she must have understood the frustration of not being able to communicate. Her response to me was always swift and loud. With perfect enunciation and tones, Natalin would repeat the desired word or phrase for me the way it should have been said. Even today, seven years later, I can hear her voice ringing in my head. She would bob her head at me, directing me to keep repeating her until I said the phrase to her satisfaction. Next this unlearned, but brilliant teacher would pick up an object on the dirt floor and begin an instructive conversation in which I would have to use my new phrase correctly.

Natalin made me excited about learning a language. Her focus was never on my inabilities, but rather on the task at hand. I not only learned Kumboi from Natalin; I learned how to teach as well. Like every good mother, I tend to think my child is exceptional. I imagine him orating to thousands and awing them with his eloquence. But this week has been enlightening for me. I look at little children with different eyes—or I should say, I hear them with different ears!

Long before our children begin "school," they are developing a propensity to learn. If that desire to learn is thwarted or denied, it might wither and die. If it is cultivated and cared for, it will doubtless grow. I have often said that homeschooling is a way of life; a way of learning. Now I believe that teaching is a way of life as well.

Rebekah's Diary can be found at www.NoGreaterJoy.org

Geography Food

We select a country, find it on the map, check out the language, and even look to see if they have a Bible in their language, or if NGJ has *Good and Evil* in that language. We pray for the people of the country at breakfast all that week. We also do a web search for food and recipes of that people group, then make a grocery list for the recipes. We talk about clothes or any other ideas to make our experience more authentic, and then on Friday night we all fix the meal together and tell Daddy what we learned.

Teach your children to become the Light of the World.
1. Go to www.iMissionaries.org
2. Choose a people group
3. Place an ad on Facebook
4. Pray together as a family for your chosen people group

Put eternity into your children's souls!

Vision

Remember, I told you of the vision that drove the pioneer homeschool families. That battle has been won for many years, yet many homeschooling families have kept hanging on to the concept that "homeschooling" is the vision—the end-game. Many think the family itself is the end-game. If that is your perspective then you are doomed to disappointment.

On the next page you will find an interview we had with a second-generation homeschooler who was raised in the thick of the "homeschool battle." For the sake of his children, his purpose has shifted to the heavenly, and it shows in the success he is seeing.

From T.J. Slayman

I say, give your children a vision from their youth. Encourage them to consider their life's ministry in the Kingdom of God. Cause their schooling to be training for that ministry.

Most homeschoolers seem to have the same limited vision as do public school children. All of their present life is focused on finishing high school. It's as if a curtain is pulled over their future and they see themselves as just students until they finish that last workbook. It is assumed they are not yet qualified to have a vision for their purpose in life. They are given little responsibility, other than that which chickens have, keeping the nest clean.

Children study certain subjects to prepare for a medical career; why not teach your little ones to think of the day when God can use them to go to a field that is white unto the harvest? Their geography class may entail following the work and needs of the missionaries on a world map. Their math class can be collecting cast-off items from other families, having a garage sale, counting the money, learning how to get a money order, and then sending it to a missionary. Their language class could be writing missionaries to tell them you have marked their place on the map and are praying for them. Give your children a vision—God's vision of reaching every tongue, kindred, and nation. Kids simply need to be asked regularly, "So what are you going to do with this life God has given you?" Whether the answer is towards ministry or some other occupation, it will at least break the mundane that seems to grip youngsters.

Foreign Language Flash Cards:
Place foreign vocabulary words on blank cards and tape the cards to the items the words represent. Makes for quick learning.

la ventana

¿Que hora es?

el horno

la maiz

la sal

la cuchara

la taza

el plato

Search   Websites and Resources

Websites and Resources for Foreign Languages

- **Edhelper**
  This site offers worksheets to learn simple words in German, French, Italian and Spanish.
  http://www.edhelper.com/Languages.htm

- **USA Reading School**
  For 16 years, the world's first free online phonics program has been teaching the foundational basics of reading to children and adults with amazing results. Extremely succesful with homeschoolers and literacy centers around the world. Over 50,000 students around the world have gone through this course.
  http://billjanaecooksey.tripod.com/Classes.html

- **PowerspeaK[12]**
  The leading world language learning provider of curriculum to schools. Designed for elementary,

middle, and high school students, these programs include intuitive games and activities that immerse you in a natural and powerful way to learn language. Fully accredited courses align to state and national standards set forth by the American Council on the Teaching of Foreign Languages.

http://www.power-glide.com/

- **The Learnables®**
  The original picture system of instruction that teaches foreign languages through use of the comprehension method.

  http://www.learnables.com/

- **Pimsleur Approach**
  Audio courses available in over 50 languages. Scientifically proven to be the most reliable way to learn a language.

  http://www.pimsleur.com

- **Rosetta Stone**

  http://www.rosettastone.com/homeschool/?cid=cjhs

Shoshanna's Reflections

Pearl Kid #5

Brownies for Dad

My older sister Shalom and I always loved playing house. Our family lived on a beautiful farm of 100 acres. We had lots of room to use our imaginations and be whatever we dreamed up. I remember this particular day quite well. We were 5 and 7, playing in the loft of my dad's shop. It was not a modern-day shop of clean, sealed walls, doors, and windows. It was made of rough-cut wood and old, used fixtures, and was open and breezy. The windows were framed holes with plastic over them. I can still smell the wood smoke that came from the stove my grandfather picked up at an auction years before. Dad is a great woodworker and was always building cabinets or chairs, or carving spoons and bowls.

That day he was hard at work as Shalom and I watched him through the cracks of the loft walls. We were giggling with great delight. We had found a whole bucket of seed corn that the squirrels and mice had been eating. It was a cold day, perfect for brownies, we thought. With mischief in our eyes, we went to work. We went up to the house and asked Mom for anything that was going bad. Our house was built better than the shop, but we always bought sale stuff, and that meant bugs were bound to be found in something out of date. With thrills of mischief, we took our goods back to the shop loft that we had converted into our playhouse. Adding a little of this and a little of that, we came up with the perfect texture. We poured it into a thin, tin baking pan. Dad had gotten a few hundred baking pans from an auction real cheap, with something else he needed. We carefully brought our pan of brownies to the house and put it in the woodstove oven. We waited impatiently while they cooked. Finally they were done! Mom helped Shalom get them out, and we called Dad in. We were so excited we could not wipe the silly grins from our faces. "Dad, we made something special for you. BROWNIES!!!!" I said. Shalom was the sweet one of the two of us, so I made her promise not to give our secret away. She would have told him in an instant. I wanted to drag it out as long as I could. We served him a brownie and stood there, eyes wide, watching him. He smiled and started to brag on what sweethearts we were. I was laughing inside so hard I could hardly stand it. In slow motion, his fork went into the brownie. He scooped it up, and it started for his mouth.

The seconds seemed like they went on forever. When the fork was just inches from his mouth, we both screamed, "STOP! Don't eat it! It is gross! The mice were in it!" We just about died laughing, knowing we could have gotten him to eat it if we had wanted him to. We all laughed and laughed! That was one of those perfect days when you just can't wipe the stupid grin off your face. LIFE IS GOOD!

~Shoshanna

"Real life is learning to cook, clean and create.
Are you homeschooling your children to succeed in real life?"
Debi

Websites and Resources for Home Economics found on pages 158-159

Debi says

2¢ "If I had another life to live, the one subject I would master is chemistry. It would be of practical value in so many areas of life, from cooking to understanding herbs, the human body, medicines, chemicals, even such things as making gunpowder and household products."

Beans, Beans

I bought several bags of dried beans and a large container to hold the beans. On cold damp days, I lay a large table cloth on the floor and the children work with the beans. Each is given a job—separate beans into color, separate into piles of 10 or 100, make pictures with beans, roads, etc. There are only two rules: (1) no throwing beans, and (2) all the beans must stay on the tablecloth. We even separated our beans so we could cook them.

Mostly Girls

We go to junk stores or yard sales and buy clothes with the idea of cutting them into squares for quilt making. At closing time, many people just give everything away. We separate matching colors and textures into piles, and then on rainy days we carefully cut out our squares. After we have a big bunch, we take pictures of the squares, put them on the computer, and piece them together to make a very pleasing color design. Brilliant gold,

bronze, and silver materials make stunning patterns.

Each of my daughters has a hope chest full of quilts and other piece-work. Other families often request squares from us, and we enjoy the opportunity to share. We have made many baby quilts for gifts. Now the girls make and sell patch skirts and bags for good prices.

As the girls grow, I can see their individual talents coming forth. One daughter is more creative; the next is a detail person and has started a line of personalized items; the youngest daughter is given to marketing. They make a great team.

Pressed Flowers

Press flowers, ferns, and leaves for making pretty stationery, wrapping paper, and cards.

Vision

A child's emotional well-being will suffer from the days that go by without the sound of laughter. How could laughter matter so much? Because laughter is love's receipt, and joy is proof that the heart is sound. Children might have no idea what is going on in the minds of their parents, but they always know what is going on in their hearts.

Hospitality Celebration

One family has turned HOSPITALITY into a learning time. The children learned that helping people in a personal way is important. In preparation for visitors they clean, wash windows, set up sleeping areas, gather extra chairs and tables, make place cards and flower arrangements, bake, and all the while sing hymns together. They learned by example that company coming is a celebration time.

2 ¢ | *"This next idea is a real keeper! Try it and see."*

Dinner

Every Friday at noon we sit at the table with the children to plan our weekly dinner menu. It would be easier to do this myself…actually, it would be easier not to even have a weekly menu, but the dividends of this homeschool project for my children have been priceless.

We discuss the pros and cons of each meal suggestion; which includes our budget, health needs, time it takes to prepare, clean-up time, particular nights when it is necessary to have a fast dinner because of church night, and then of special interest is the family night party which includes fun foods.

While we make the list of meals, one of the older children creates a grocery list with all the other children reminding her of what she might have missed. Then we discuss what can be made ahead of time, including bread, etc. Everyone has a say in who helps with which meal. The assigned helpers are listed on the calendar. All this takes about 30 minutes.

Our whole family (me too) is now trained to plan ahead. It is an excellent Proverbs 31 habit. This weekly habit has brought unexpected rewards. The grocery bill is considerably less, and our meals are much healthier. There are no stressful days where I draw a blank on what to cook for dinner. It brings total peace to the dinner table because even the children who didn't vote for that meal know the next meal is their choice, so they gladly partake of their siblings' meals. The most important thing it does is cause the family, even the small children, to feel they are a part of what makes the family tick. It also teaches them how to cook, clean up as you go, and it gives them an opportunity to be with Mom in this cherished time.

The children have a working idea of budget, which really cuts down on begging. Other moms marvel at how wise our children seem when we are out together and a question comes up about stopping by for ice cream or some other expensive and unhealthy treat.

Vision

The early homeschool pioneers were blessed with a total lack of curriculum. There was simply nothing from which to choose. Life was so much less confusing. Moms were forced to get creative. There were no guidelines, no directions, and no dreary workbooks to steal away reality. Children learned hands-on. There were no YouTube videos or video games, and that was good and bad. I love learning from YouTube videos.

Cleaning Fun

We had difficulty getting our children motivated to keep their room tidy. I was always fussing and often there was conflict which spoiled our mornings; and the bad spirit (mom and kids) spilled over into our school time. Not anymore.

We devised a plan. Every morning before breakfast the children clean up their rooms and let me know when they are ready for "inspection." As inspector, I come to their room as a historical figure: General Patton, Louis Armstrong, Adam, Moses, King David, Esther, or whoever strikes my fancy. After passing the inspection the children race to our old encyclopedias and look up the person to find out more facts. We did this for weeks until the habit of cleaning their rooms was well established. Then we moved on to another exciting new game or project. The secret with keeping children fascinated is change. Never do one thing until they are tired of it.

Jeremiah James and Penelope Jane, our little entrepreneurs.

Seedling Sale

Transplanting Seedlings & Growing Plants
by Shoshanna (Pearl) Easling

Seedlings are ready to transplant as soon as they start to grow their second leaf. Transplanting seedlings is quite fun! You see the seed germinate. It grows into a sprout that becomes a seedling. You take care of it and watch it get strong and healthy. It is amazing to see life come from a tiny, hard seed growing out of the soil and into the world. I cannot help but be amazed at the intricate details of God's creation!

Okay, I am getting carried away with the artistic side of Creation. Let's get back to transplanting our seedling.

Mix Plant-tone granular fertilizer into your potting soil if desired. Fill containers with potting soil, but do not pack.

1. Pull up a whole clump of seedlings and disturb roots.

2. Pull seedlings apart.

3. Poke hole in the middle of a pot and plant seedling, being careful not to break the stem.

4. Water with full-strength fish solution or compost tea until soil is thoroughly moistened.

Biscuit Time!

The Well
by Debi Pearl

I have very fond memories of my grandmother training me in the art of making biscuits. Teaching me seemed to make her happy. Each morning she would pull out the biscuit board that was built into the cabinet. It was a board, like a table top, mounted like a drawer. It was always covered with flour. Once the board was extended, she would mound two cups of flour on it. Then she would explain to me as she pushed a hole in the middle of the flour, "First, make your well." The "well" was just a hole in the middle of the pile of flour. To my young ears, calling the hole a "well" sounded so fine—mysterious-like. Into the well she dumped slightly warm lard, and then added homemade buttermilk. With her thumb and index finger, working only in the well, she worked the lard and buttermilk, gradually incorporating the flour until it formed a soft dough. She rolled the dough with a rolling pin a few times, and then patted it down to about a half-inch thick. With her biscuit cutter she pressed out about ten biscuits. She always had a big black skillet with butter in it warming in the oven. Each biscuit would quickly be turned in the warmed butter before she added the next one. While they baked in her hot oven, I played with the leftover dough, learning how to cut out biscuits. I can clearly remember standing there, almost eye-level with the countertop, working with the dough while drinking in the wonderful aroma of baking biscuits.

My grandmother trained me to make biscuits. She trained me to laugh while making biscuits. My mischievous streak was developed in that kitchen as I conferred with my grandmother about how we could scare Papa when he came in for breakfast.

> **M**any parents get so worked up over making their children be obedient, they forget that training doesn't mean discipline; it means instructing the child in how to master the issues of life.

Ask my staff—I am well-trained in making biscuits and in the art of scaring distracted office workers. I am the queen of "BOO!"

Oh, how dearly I loved my grandmother! As I look back, I know I must have left her floor covered with flour, yet she included me. I can't remember a time I disobeyed my grandmother. I wanted to please her.

Today, I sat at the kitchen table making guacamole out of 600 avocados. You read it correctly…*600* avocados. A man in the church was able to buy a hundred boxes of avocados for a ridiculously low price. I bought ten boxes from him. My daughter Shoshanna and 3-year-old granddaughter Penelope dropped by while I was in the middle of my green venture. Penelope didn't hesitate a minute. She was up in my lap, and where once there were two hands working, suddenly there were four. She imitated my every move. It slowed me down considerably, and green goo plopped on the floor a few times, but her joy in helping was immeasurable; and more important, she was being trained to love to work with her hands. It was Proverbs 31—Training Class 101.

Training is the art of imparting skill sets and worldviews. Training a child "in the way he should go" involves taking a child by the hand and allowing him to be a part of your productive life. If you cook a meal and don't have your little girl standing beside you as you talk her through every step of the process, then you are NOT training her up to be a good cook. If you clean house, shop, sew, have Bible studies, or any number of productive activities, and you don't involve your children, then you are not TRAINING UP your children in the way they should go.

God stated it correctly when he said, "Train up a child in the way he should go, and when he is old he will not depart from it." When you train a child to enjoy cooking, she will always enjoy cooking. When you train up a child to work, he will always enjoy the accomplishment of a job well done. When you train up a child to notice what needs to be done, to be on time, to be respectful, to work as a team, to use time wisely, and to put his shoulder to the plow, he will always be responsible and productive.

It is not a strange turn of events that one boy grows up to be lazy while another is a worker; that one woman is bitter and the other is full of joy; that one person is productive and the other expects others to pay his way; that one man is lustful and the other is self-disciplined; that one woman is emotionally crippled and the other is wise and thoughtful.

Train up—not spank up or fuss up or even instruct up—it is TRAIN UP. Train her how to make biscuits. It starts with a well and results in a life well lived.

"Train up a child in the way he should go: and when he is old, he will not depart from it" (Proverbs 22:6).

2¢ | "Creativity is far more viable than knowledge. It has no limits or boundaries. Creativity will take you beyond the status quo; knowledge alone will not even qualify you for hourly wages."

The Flower House
by Shalom (Pearl) Brand

When I was a little girl, my sister and I played house all day, every day. We would build our play-pretend houses everywhere we went. I remember days when Dad would come in from work and stop and stare in shock at the mess Shoshanna and I had made in the sunroom. We would take every book, chair, cushion, cardboard, or blanket that Mom would let us use and build ourselves a fancy home.

One time we found a pile of old flowers the graveyard keeper had tossed over the fence onto our farm. With great excitement we took them to our yard and stuck them into the ground to create flower walls for our house. We thought it was so wonderful. We ran to find Dad and Mom so they could come and see our wonderful new house. With great pleasure and pride we showed it off. Like the fine parents they are, they smiled and sat at a makeshift table in our magnificent flower kitchen room and pretended to eat with us.

I look back to my childhood and realize that when my parents saw the plastic flowers all over the front lawn they must have been thinking, "Oh, no! What a mess!" But as a child I never had a clue that our flower playhouse was anything but beautiful. To them, their smart little girls only filled their hearts with gladness.

The first year of my marriage, I lived in a magical world of making a real house become a special home. A pleasure and pride very akin to what I knew as a child daily filled my heart. When Dad and Mom came over to visit, I fed them real food at a real table, and it was so much fun.

Last night, my good husband brought home some short pieces of wood from his job. My two little girls found them, and right now, as I am writing this, both are outside gleefully making a new playhouse with the small pieces of wood and some fake flowers left over from a party. When they are finished making their playhouse, like my mother before me, I will go out and sit with them in their kitchen and pretend to eat dirt cake. And someday when my daughters are married, with the same pride that they once fed me dirt cake, they will feed me fine foods at their real table. They will, as I have done, reflect back to the glorious days of their childhood, remembering that Mama took time to play pretend with them.

" This is an excellent rainy day project and a good gift idea. Did you know that at most newspaper offices, you can get, for free or for a very low cost, a remnant roll of newprint paper?"

Recipe Book

Most libraries have a sale room where you can obtain out-of-date cooking magazines at a very low cost—or sometimes free. I pick up a few each time I go to the library. As we get the magazines, we look through them, placing different-colored paper stickers to identify the kind of recipes that catch our eye. A gray tab means it is a main dish recipe that has meat in it, yellow stands for beans, green for salad, pink for desert, etc. Each of the children has a new photo album they are using to create their personal cookbook. Once a month, we go through our magazines and each child cuts out a few recipes and pictures they like best to add to their own photo book. One of my daughters is making a cake cookbook, the next daughter (more health-conscious) a salad cookbook, and the older daughter is making a cookbook for meat dishes. This year, the children are making recipe books they will give as a gift to someone special. They really love doing this because they see me using my recipe book which we built together last year. They also see that I am always adding new recipes or taking out old recipes that I no longer like. Besides this, once a month each of the children chooses a recipe to cook for the family (with my help). If we all like the dish, then it is a keeper for the family recipe book; if it is not so good, we pull the recipe out of the picture slot to discard. My children are becoming good cooks while making great memories; the recipe books they give as gifts to Grandma and Auntie will be their legacy.

BIG Family Solutions
Dot-to-Dot Kids

I have 6 sons. Sons have a tendency to grow…quickly. To keep track of their clothes, I put one dot on clothes that belong to the oldest. When he outgrows his and they are passed down to the next son, I add a second dot because the second son has two dots on his clothes. If his are passed down to my third son…you guessed it, I just add another dot. I use the dot system for school books as well as other belongings. When I see six dots I know who the item belongs to, and most important, they know.

Nurse's Chart

For years I was a RN in a very busy hospital. Now I am a very busy homeschooling mom of eight, children ranging from 4 to 15 years old. At the hospital, we always put up our assignment on a dry-erase board, so everyone knew what was expected of them and of others. I use the same technique at home.

Each morning, I quickly mark down beside each child's name basic duties, homeschool pages and any other needed information. At a glance they know what is expected of them right at the start of the day. It brings a lot of peace to the family.

Megan
- Get up. Get dressed. Make bed. Tidy room.
- 6:30 AM — Eat breakfast. Bible study.
- 7:00 AM — Dishes. Table. Counter top. Stove. rugs. sweep. mop.
- ~ 8:30 AM — Eat Lunch. Dishes. Table. Countertop. Stove. rugs. Sweep. mop.
- 12:00 - 1:30 PM — Eat Supper. Dishes. Table. Counter top. stove. rugs. sweep. mop.
- 5:00 - 6:00 PM — Shower. Brush teeth. Floss. Bedtime: 9:00 PM
- 8:00 PM — WEEKLY CLEANING: dusting. sweep/mop. windows

Organization for Sanity

Until you have several small children you can't imagine how confusing life can get. After having six children in seven years, we had to get organized. I made a chart with each child's photo on the chart. Each child has a particular color sippy cup. Beside their chart photo is a picture of their sippy cup. When I put four sippy cups on the table even the 10-month-old fastens onto her color cup without hesitation. Their blanket and pillows match their cups. I even started buying shirts and socks to match the cups so there is no confusion.

A small basket under their bed holds their PJs during the day, and when they are tucked in at night I place the next day's clothes into their baskets; so even the two-year-old can get up and take his PJs off and put his clothes on, with a little help from his big sister.

I moved the dressers into the laundry room so I could quickly fold and put away the clothes, and I can take everybody's clothes out at the same time, ready for the next day. It also gives their bedroom more space for playing.

Everywhere we go each child has their own certain place at the table in the order they have been assigned. Each one has their own small chores to do at the same time everyone else does theirs.

We keep the recorder and a stack of books by the beanbag. The phone ringing is a signal to the little ones to head to the beanbag. While the five-year-old grabs the prepared bowl of pretzels, the six-year-old turns on the recorder and sits down as the leader. "Huddle" is the word we use to cause everyone to sit at their designated spot and face big brother who shows the book to the rest and turns on the recorder. It is a sight to behold. My friends marvel at my clean house and lack of being frazzled. I just say, "First organize and then all that is left is to manage…" I read it in the Pearls' book, *Training Children to Be Strong in Spirit.*

Buddy Up

When my third child was born, I handed him to my oldest and said, "This is your buddy." Ten children later…the buddy system is still working. For every chore the older buddy always has a *little helper*. The younger child is expected to show respect and obey their "Big Buddy." This provokes the older children to be protective of the younger siblings; and having responsibility seems to help the children be mature and sober-minded earlier. From morning dressing and breakfast to tucking in at night, the older sibling is playing the role of big buddy to their charge. On occasion, Dad will take the Big Buddies out for a special bowling and pizza night, leaving the "Little Buddies" at home with Mama until they are Big Buddies. People marvel at how well our children get along. I learned early that when the younger children can force the older children to *do their bidding* by crying and telling Mama, it will cause the older children to dislike their younger siblings. They will resent the young ones. And WHY not? But when the younger children are expected to treat their older siblings with respect, and even obey them, then the older children like their younger brothers and sisters.

Simple logic. *Great* plan.

Vision

We have "work parties." Work and party are not supposed to go together; but then, we are homeschoolers aren't we? ☺

Shelling peas, cleaning house, and gardening become enjoyable events by adding a little imagination, and of course competition, with a nice reward waiting for the worker with the most willing hands. The name "party" helps to set the tone.

What is venison?

Cooking Skills

My children, from 9 to 15 years old, girls and boys, take a night each week to cook a meal. We all sit down together with pencil in hand, we list what each will cook, make a grocery list, and then decide how long it will take to cook the meal. One son likes to grill everything. Another likes to cook breakfast. We live on a tight budget, so it can be a challenge for them to plan and cook a meal to their liking for such a limited amount of money.

Families that volunteer are well liked. Being liked counts for a lot. Volunteer children grow up feeling like they are needed by other people—again, a big plus. Children actively volunteering learn self-discipline and become ready to give an answer without being shy or backward. Add it all up and it makes volunteering one of the most valuable outlets of homeschooling.

"Finch Family Volunteers"

1. Homeschoolers are known for being first-class volunteers. We made our family available at a local Civil War site (Battle of Richmond) and participate in their "School Days."

2. All four of my kids help give the tours at Waveland State Historic Site during the public school tours. Imagine how shocked the school students/teachers are at the homeschooler's knowledge about the place! The kids loved this.

3. The older kids volunteer at a pet clinic to gain a better understanding of pet care (even getting to watch the surgeries...talk about anatomy!) How cool is that?

4. We serve the community by volunteering at a local nursing home and taking "church" to the old folks. Our 15-year-old leads the studies as the younger children play music and do skits for the residents.

Also, teaching children to see those that serve them as worthy of their hire is teaching good character, thus will translate into thankfulness in every area of their lives. God loves this kind of heart. It is a parent's job to give the child this vision of seeing those that serve as worthy of appreciation.

Debi says

2¢ "Pay attention, moms; this simple idea can translate over into a multitude of areas.
It could change your children's entire lives!"

The Mailbox Express

At the beginning of each school year we make mailboxes out of oatmeal containers. Everyone paints their own container, makes a flag that moves up and down, and puts their name and address on it. Then we secure the container to a thin board. The rule is that only good things arrive in our mailbox.

Each day, I put a small note or a simple gift for each child. Often I would leave a poem that was only partially written, with lines for them to complete, or maybe a half-drawn picture for them to finish. They also received their weekly chore list and their weekly rewards. In my box I often find notes of love and small pieces of rocks or feathers. All the children look for things they can add to my box or to each other's boxes. Daddy leaves a piece of candy on occasion, so we all especially enjoy getting mail from him.

Soon they will be too old for such things; but the older children like to bless the little ones, so I guess it will continue on for a while yet. It is our family tradition which the children have enjoyed explaining to visitors. It makes us special.

Slow No More

My son used to drag around all morning doing his chores, which pushed back the time when he started his day's schooling. I made one simple change in our schedule. I listed his chores on the fridge, then told him that as soon as they were complete he would have his breakfast. Each morning, I make a quick check before he sits down to eat. It is amazing; what once took him hours now takes only minutes, and I never have to push him. His growling tummy keeps him motivated. This simple self-motivation has changed his habits in every area. I realized that I had been conditioning him to be a slacker; now I condition him to be jolly fast and efficient.

Child Care
Taking Care of Jewell

When I started homeschooling, I had three children ready for school and a baby girl named Jewell. At first, I would ask one of the children to take care of Jewell while I tried to do my housework or homeschool the other two children. It was always, "Oh, Mama, do I have to? I'm busy. I did it last time." Then one day, I had the children help me make a "Jewell Chart." It was just empty blocks with a packet of colored stars. When you took care of her you put a star in the block. At a glance it was easy to see whose color was next, and the children enjoyed putting up the stars. We also stated what each child would teach Jewell when their time rolled around. This gave extra reading out loud as the children "taught" the baby. Sounds simple, but it proved to be remarkably helpful.

nogreaterjoy.org

No Greater Joy   iMissionaries   Good and Evil   CreatedtobehisHelpmeet   Preparingto...hisHelpmeet   Bulk Herb Store

No Greater Joy Ministries – Family Magazine, Child Training Articles, Marriage Resources, Bible Teaching Videos from...

Search   Websites and Resources

Websites and Resources for Home Economics

Cooking

- **Snowman Peppermint White Hot Chocolate**
  Makes 2 servings.
    - 2 cups milk
    - 2 — 4 peppermint herbal tea bags (use 2 for light peppermint flavor and 4 for stronger flavor)
    - 4 ounces good quality white chocolate, coarsely chopped
    - Whipped cream, for garnish
    - White chocolate curls, for garnish.
  http://www.lafujimama.com/2012/01/peppermint-white-hot-chocolate/
- **Ice Cream Cone Cupcakes**
  http://mom.me/food/3908-ice-cream-cone-cupcakes
- **Blueberry Buckwheat Pancakes**

http://mom.me/food/
3912-blueberry-buckwheat-pancakes/

- **25 Tips for coking with kids**
  http://b-inspiredmama.com/2012/05/
  25-tips-for-cooking-with-kids-from/

Sewing

- **Skip to my Lou**
  This site is full of useful ideas and techniques to teach your children the basics of sewing.
  http://www.skiptomylou.org/2013/03/05/sewing-activities-for-kids/

- **Kids Apron Set**
  Super cute apron, pot holders, and oven mitt patterns.(will fit sizes 2-6).
  http://sew-whats-new.com/forum/topics/

  kids-apron-set-free-pattern-apron-two-pot-holders-one-oven-mitt

- **Sewing 4 Fun**
  First year sewing projects for kids.
  http://sewing4fun.com/first-year-sewing-projects-for-kids/

- **16 easy sewing crafts for kids.**
  http://b-inspiredmama.com/2012/08/easy-to-sew-gifts-for-kids/

Nathan's Quest

Pearl Kid #3

Did you know that God gave each believer a life-long job? That's right! Christ said in Mark 16:15, "And he said unto them, Go ye into all the world, and preach the gospel to every creature." We have a mission. Male or female, child or grandparent, YOU have a mission. What are you going to do about it?

God tells us the story of a life-long job he had for a man named Moses: being a leader to millions of people. One day Moses was walking on a hill with his father-in-law's sheep when he saw a burning bush that just kept burning. This was curious. Moses stopped to take a look, and suddenly the voice of God came out of the bush and told Moses that it was God speaking to him, so he needed to take his shoes off and listen carefully. "I have surely seen the affliction of my people which are in Egypt, and have heard their cry by reason of their taskmasters; for I know their sorrows; And I am come down to deliver them out of the hand of the Egyptians…Come now therefore, and I will send thee unto Pharaoh, that thou mayest bring forth my people the children of Israel out of Egypt."

Even though this was the voice of God speaking to him through a bush, the only thing Moses could say was, "I can't do that! I stutter; I can't be a speaker. You must have the wrong guy." Three different times God spoke to Moses of his lifetime job, and each time Moses had an excuse for why he was not the right choice. Finally Moses accepted his mission and did all the LORD told him to do.

God needed a man who had a heart to love and honor him. He needed a man who would turn to God in prayer, asking what he should do. Moses could use others to help him, but the leadership of Israel needed to be from a man who would seek God's face.

Fast forward thousands of years to the time when Jesus was giving all those who love him his final instructions: "Thus it is written, and thus it behoved Christ to suffer, and to rise from the dead the third day: And that repentance and remission of sins should be preached in his name among all nations, beginning at Jerusalem" (Luke 24:46-47).

Jesus has given all of us lifetime jobs. Jesus, the beloved Son of God, suffered the indignity of death to redeem us. Then he gave us our job of a lifetime, "TELL everyone about Jesus."

It is not about your abilities. It is about your willingness.

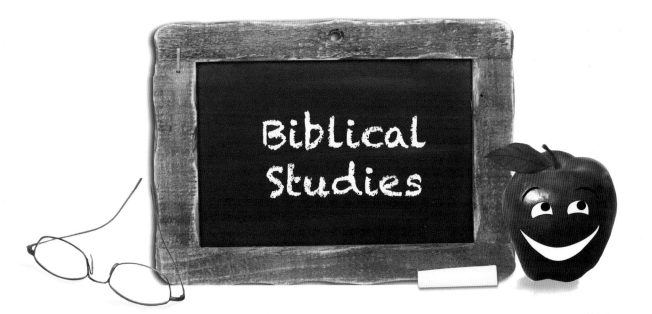

Biblical Studies

"God chose to reveal who He is, not by teaching principles or ideas but by producing a history book on how he related to His people."

Debi

Biographies of Great Christian Missionaries and Faith found on pages 174-175

Websites and Resources for Biblical Studies found on pages 176-177

Who Am I?

Each week the children draw a picture illustrating one of the stories in the Bible, and the rest of us try to figure out which story it is. We get quite competitive, which means they might spend considerable time reading the Bible, trying to come up with a really great story. When we fail to figure out the story that goes with the picture, as a group we read the story together. Then the other children draw all the art.

Training a Leader

The book of Proverbs has 31 chapters. We read through the book of Proverbs each month, one chapter each day. The children take turns reading a verse. Mom helps the baby "read" hers, and the oldest child helps the two-year-old read his, etc. When the older children read, they stand across the room and read to an "audience." This is our public speaking class. (The Pearl family did this too.)

I cannot communicate adequately how desperately children need to see their parents laugh and love each other. Emotional health begins with knowing the people around you are all right. I've known families who were absolute heathen, yet raised happy, stable children because of the healthy atmosphere at home. Family devotions and religious rebukes don't produce healthy souls; healthy souls produce healthy souls!

Memory Game

When we go shopping, the children take turns assuming responsibility to remember where we parked the car. At the mall, they have to remember which store we came through to get into the mall. It is a fun challenge which they enjoy and discuss among themselves. It is a simple way to make them observant and instill responsibility.

Thankfulness is key to honoring God, worshiping God, and serving God. It paves the road to a wholesome life, a restful life, a peaceful life—a happy life. Being thankful is an ACT of the will, something you CHOOSE. It is making a conscious decision that God is worthy and should be praised and thanked no matter what the circumstance. When we have that attitude toward God, we stop having a critical attitude toward others. We look at every event as an occasion for learning.

1 KINGS 17:17-24

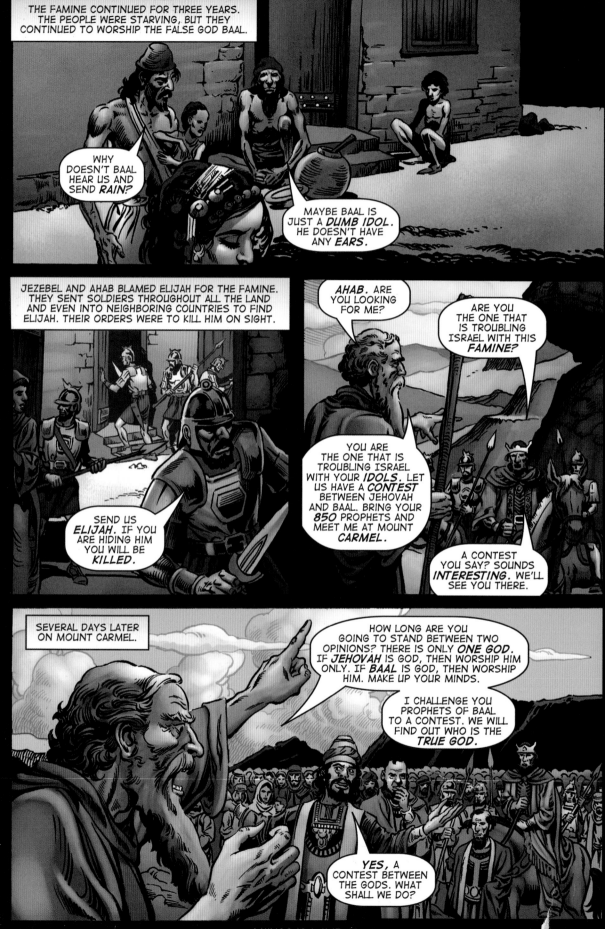

1 KINGS 18:1, 4 17-21

Michael tells a tale: Of Utmost Concern...

I think most of you feel as do I about many common issues. My most important personal concern is my children.

Even before I was married, my occupation, financial security, ministry and personal fulfillment all took third place to concerns for my future children. "What does it profit a man if he gain the whole world and lose his own soul?" Likewise, what does it profit if a father gains the whole world but loses the souls of his children?

What can be called success if your children turn out to be part of the world's problem rather than its cure? What satisfaction can there be in the comforts of material success if your children grow up needing counsel rather than being sought out to give counsel? If your children lie awake at night suffering from guilt and anxiety, being gnawed upon by the demons of intemperance and self-indulgence, how can you enjoy your food or your pillow?

The success of a tree and a man is measured by the fruit that is borne. The fruit of a man or woman is their children; everything else is falling leaves. If the sun rises and sets and I never cast a bigger shadow, what of it, if my children are growing and flourishing in God's family?

Let me die poor; let me die early; let me be ravaged by disease; just let my children rise up and call me blessed. Let me not measure my giving by the dollars I spend on them or the educational opportunities that my station in life affords them, but rather, by the hours I spend with them in fellowship.

May they graduate from my tutorship to become disciples of the Man from Nazareth. May they learn good and evil from the pinnacle of obedience rather than from the pit of despair. May they have the wisdom to choose the precious, and the courage to reject the trite and the vain in life. May they always labor for the meat that endures. May they be lovers of God, coworkers with the Holy Spirit, and a friend to the Lord Jesus. And when their trail ends, may it end at the throne of God, laying crowns at the Savior's feet.

2¢ "Thanksgiving is an outpouring of the very root of the soul. It is a reflection of the heart. It reveals peace. It is the presence of goodwill toward others."

Lesson on JOY
by Debi Pearl

When my oldest daughter was about 12 years old, I suddenly woke up to the fact that she lacked joy in her life. As a young mother, I wanted her to be happy, to thrive, and to find great contentment in creativity, but I had no idea how to make this happen. One day, I was reading aloud Psalm 30:9–12 when I noticed my younger children dancing around with their hands in the air. I glanced down and read again, "What profit is there in my blood, when I go down to the pit? Shall the dust praise thee? shall it declare thy truth? Hear, O LORD, and have mercy upon me: LORD, be

thou my helper. Thou hast turned for me my mourning into dancing: thou hast put off my sackcloth, and girded me with gladness; To the end that my glory may sing praise to thee, and not be silent. O LORD my God, I will give thanks unto thee for ever."

That day I set up a homeschool project for my daughter. She was to find all the words in the Bible that were connected with the word JOY. Over the next few weeks, her notebook was filled with verses on thanksgiving, dancing, laughter, sacrifice, and gladness. She taught me as she studied. What impressed me more than anything was the fact that thanksgiving was a sacrifice of praise and worship. Sacrifice—something I did that was not a natural happening. The opposite would also stand true. Being down-in-the-mouth was unthankfulness, which would be an insult toward God. I have a naturally upbeat personality, but there were times when I was stressed and I immediately recognized it as what it was—unthankfulness.

Bitterness is a very troublesome word and certainly a taxing state of mind.

So I asked myself, what is a source of stress or ingratitude in my life? Sometimes it is a simple thing, such as being under too much pressure to perform—basically, too much to do with too little energy to see it through. Mike always says life is better if you organize and manage. Hiring a young girl to help homeschool, clean house, and cook helped me get focused on important issues. I traded vegetables with her mother because we didn't have money to spare for paying a helper. The results were wonderful. As my daughter continued her study on joy, I continued to search my life for ways I could dwell on thanksgiving. God began a work in both of us; really, our whole family benefited from this study. The word of God was quick and powerful in our lives as we sought to honor God through being thankful. For some people, the issue of unthankfulness runs much deeper. I must admit after all these years of counseling that my first thought when I think of an unthankful person is that bitterness has taken root.

Bitterness is a very troublesome word and certainly a taxing state of mind. The worst thing about bitterness is that it is so catchy. It is like the pandemic flu that all health officials dread. Some people spend their whole life in a state of bitterness and never recognize it for what it is. They are just vexed in their souls about so-and-so or this-or-that.

Bitterness causes a person to perceive hurt. Hebrews 12:15 says, "Looking diligently lest any man fail of the grace of God; lest any root of bitterness springing up trouble you, and thereby many be defiled." God says look diligently, because it takes real focus to avoid catching the flu of bitterness.

Bitterness does not allow the brain to ever really rest. A bitter person's mind is forever devising contrived conversations that will convince everyone how terribly she has been treated. These unsavory thoughts spill out, defiling those around you. It is sad how bitterness defiles whole families, following generation after generation.

Bitterness never stays put; it eventually spreads to taint how you react to your

spouse, fellow worker or boss, and folks at church; as you raise your children, you will become bitter toward them and they toward you. They grow up viewing life through your bitter, ungrateful eyes. Sleep eludes the bitter soul. Restless nights give evidence of a troubled mind and an unthankful heart. Don't let bitterness eat away all that is joyful and good in your life. Take a good look at yourself instead of looking at others, and declare war on unthankfulness.

God's WORD is effectual. It is alive and working, able to change you as you study it. Open your Bible and do a study on joy or thankfulness. Look up every time the words appear, and list the words it is coupled with. Then begin to choose thankfulness—all day, every day. Practice saying thank you to God. When you feel sad, mad, depressed, or irritated, STOP and (out loud) thank God that he is able to change your heart and break this chain of unthankfulness.

Our lives are meant to be filled with joy, gladness, thankfulness, and rejoicing. It is praise to God for us to live our lives in this state. Anything less is… well, we will not go there. Enough said. *Rejoice;* and again I say, *rejoice.*

Biographies of Missionaries & Men of Faith

Suggested by Bobbie Sue

- **The Young Learner's Bible Storybook** by Mary Manz Simon. **Ages 4 & up.**
- **These are my People: The story of Gladys Aylward** by Mildred T. Howard. **Ages 8 & up.**
- **With Darling Faith: A Biography of Amy Carmichael** (focuses on her early years) by Rebecca Davis. **Ages 12 & up.**
- **Hero Tales: A Family Treasury of True Stories from the Lives of Christian Heroes** by Dave & Neta Jackson. **Ages 8 & up.**
- **Evidence Not Seen** by Darlene Deibler Rose. **Ages 15 & up.**
- ***Vanya** by Myrna Grant.
- ***Reckless Faith** by Beth Guckenberger. **Ages 13 & up.**
- ***Bonhoeffer** by Eric Metaxas.
- ***Which None Can Shut** by Reema Goode. **Ages 8 & up.**
- ***Hearts of Fire: Eight Women in the Underground Church and Their Stories of Costly Faith** by The Voice of the Martyrs.
- ***God's Smuggler** by Brother Andrew. **Ages 12 & up.**
- ***Bruchko** by Bruce Olson. **15 & up.**
- ***Cowboy Boots In Darkest Africa** by Bill Rice. **Ages 12 & up.**
- **A Path Not lined with Roses** by Peter Rumachik.
- ***The Savage My Kinsman** by Elisabeth Elliot.
- ***God's Secret Agent** by Sammy Tippit and Jerry B. Jenkins.
- ***Kisses From Katie** by Katie Davis.
- ***The Hiding Place** by Corrie Ten Boom.
- **Signing Through the Night** by Anneke Companjen.
- ***No Greater Love** by Levi Benkert.
- **Five Chimneys: The Story of Auschwitz** by Olga Lengyel.
- ***Nicholas Winton and the Rescued Generation: Save one Life, Save the World** by Muriel Emanuel.
- **If I Perish** by Esther Ahn Kim.
- **I Dared to Call Him Father: The Miraculous Story of a Muslim Woman's Encounter with God** by Bilquis Sheikh.
- **Secret Believers: What Happens When Muslims Believe in Christ** by Brother Andrew.
- ***Christian Heroes: Then & Now Book Series** (39 total) **Ages 10 & up.**

- ***Sower Series: Biography series of people of faith. Ages 9 & up.**
- **Mary Slessor** (Women of Faith Series) by Basil Miller.
- **Corrie Ten Boom** (Women of Faith Series) by Kathleen White.
- **Amy Carmichael** (Women of Faith Series) by Kathleen White.
- **Jim Elliot** (Men of Faith Series) by Kathleen White.
- **Isobel Kuhn: The Canadian Girl Who Felt God's Call to the Lisu People of China** (Women of Faith Series) by Lois Dick.
- **Gladys Aylward: The Courageous English Missionary Whose Life Defied All Expectations** (Women Of Faith Series) by Catherine Swift.
- **John Newton: The British Slave Trader Who Found Amazing Grace** (Men of Faith Series) by Catherine Swift.
- **William Carey** (Men of Faith Series) by Basil Miller.
- **John Wesley** (Men of Faith Series) by Basil Miller.
- **George Muller: Man of Faith and Miracles** (Men of Faith series) by Basil Miller.
- **Hudson Taylor** (Men of Faith Series) by J. Hudson Taylor.
- **Jonathan Goforth** (Men of Faith Series) by Rosalind Goforth.
- **Charles Spurgeon** (Men of Faith Series) by Kathy Triggs.
- **Samuel Morris: The African Boy God Sent to Prepare an American University for It's Mission to the World** (Men of Faith Series) by Lindley Baldwin.
- **Nothing Daunted: Isobel Kuhn** by Gloria Repp. **Ages 12 & up.**
- **Sojourner Truth: American Abolitionist** (Heroes of the Faith) by W. Terry Whalin.
- **Mother Teresa: Missionary of Charity** (Heroes of the Faith) by Sam Wellman. **Ages 12 & up.**
- **Charles Finney: The Great Revivalist** (Heroes of the Faith) by Bonnie Harvey.
- **D.L. Moody: The American Evangelist** (Heroes of the Faith) by Bonnie C. Harvey.
- **George Whitefield: Pioneering Evangelist** (Heroes of the Faith) by Bruce Fish.
- **David Livingstone** (Heroes of the Faith) by Sam Wellman.
- **Peace Child: An Unforgettable Story of Primitive Jungle Treachery in the 20th Century** by Don Richardson.
- ***Brother Sheffey: A Christian Who Knew the Power of Prayer** by Willard Sanders Barbery. **Ages 16 & up.**
- **Amy Carmichael of Dohnavur** by Frank Houghton. **Ages 15 & up.**
- **Mimosa: A True Story** by Amy Carmichael. **Ages 16 & up.**
- **A Father's Promise** by Donnalynn Hess. **Ages 9 & up.**

* means a great book to read aloud.

No Greater Joy Ministries – Family Magazine, Child Training Articles,

nogreaterjoy.org

No Greater Joy   iMissionaries   Good and Evil   CreatedtobehisHelpmeet   Preparingto...hisHelpmeet   Bulk Herb Stor

No Greater Joy Ministries – Family Magazine, Child Training Articles, Marriage Resources, Bible Teaching Videos from...

Search   Websites and Resources

Websites and Resources for Biblical Studies

- **Printable coloring pages**
  This site has a ton of printable coloring pages covering the days of creation. Bible stories plus ideas for crafts.
  http://www.coloring.ws/creation.htm
- **Explorer Bible Study** Good Bible curriculum for you and your family to grow through.
  http://www.explorerbiblestudy.org
- **ABC Jesus Loves Me**
  God has given each of us a huge responsibility to train the precious children in our lives. Here is a Bible-based curriculum with a solid academic foundation.
  http://www.abcjesuslovesme.com/1st-things-1st
- **Bible Based Homeschooling**
  The place to share budget friendly Bible-based resources, articles about Bible based homeschooling, and tips.
  http://biblebasedhomeschooling.com/my-vision/

- **Heart of Wisdom homeschooling worksheets.**
  Hundreds of free pages to download or read that help you bring up your children in the ways of the Lord.
  http://www.heartofwisdom.com/homeschoollinks/worksheets/
- **CARM**
  A 501(c)3 non-profit Christian ministry dedicated to the glory of the Lord Jesus Christ and the promotion and defense of the Christian Gospel, doctrine and theology.
  http://carm.org/
- **Puritans' curriculum**
  Free homeschool curriculum consistent with the historic reformed Biblical faith as it is excellently summarized in the original Westminster Standards and the Three Forms of Unity.
  http://www.puritans.net/curriculum/
- **Bible Curriculum; Rooted and Grounded & Discovering our Amazing God!**
  Written by former missionaries to Papua New Guinea.
  http://deeperroots.com/about-us/
- **Positive Action Bible Curriculum**
  https://positiveaction.org/school

Memories

Homeschool Kid—Sing My Song
Pearl Kid #1

Small children love to be identified, "You're a carpenter; you fixed my chair!" Or, "Those are good brownies; you're our little cook." Just today, my son re-adjusted a faulty toy and announced to his Mama Pearl that he is a mechanic, "because he fixes stuff."

Some parents are better at bestowing loving identities on their children than others, but all of us have given our children identities that shape them. What do you remember being called as a child?

My mom called me a good writer. I'm still wearing that particular nametag with all the joy my eight-year-old self felt when she first called me that. She also told me I would be a good wife and mama. Not only were those identities given with grand honor, they were accompanied with the tools to help them come true. Practical skills came hand-in-hand with the glorious titles we sought to earn.

One of my children's favorite ways of being "identified" by Mama is with her own personal songs. When each child is born, I make up a song that is theirs alone. "Oh, there was a little boy, and his name was Joe; Joseph—Joseph Courage! He was strong as a lion, and brave as a bear; Joseph—Joseph Courage!"

Just hearing his song makes Joe Courage square his skinny shoulders and stomp around the house with his tough-man face on. Then Rysha climbs in my lap, snuggles her head right beneath my chin, and starts humming to let me know that she wants to hear her song too.

"Ryshoni Joy, joy, my joy; Ryshoni Joy, you're beautiful…
Just like a song, song, glad song; just like a song, you're beautiful…
Just like a flower, flower, bright flower; just like a flower, you're beautiful!"

Then, as if I had just accomplished an award-winning performance, Joe and Rysha both pat me lovingly while three-year-old Joe announces, "Mom… you're… you're a good woman!"

Music

Music gives a soul to the universe, wings to the mind, flight to the imagination, and life to everything."

Plato

 Websites and Resources for Music found on pages 198-199

Sing Your Name...

Singing has been a key part of our homeschooling. Every child learned how to spell their name about the same time they learned to talk by having music added to the spelling. They learned to count money, count numbers, spell difficult words, and all kinds of beginning things. We sing hymns all day long. The Sound of Music is a regular around here. Even my children's friends call and ask if we have a song by which to learn the states, or the presidents, a particular Bible verse, a list of the bones of the body, or whatever. Music sticks...I mean it really sticks. There are expensive curriculums that use music to teach all kinds of facts. We just make up a song when we need one to remember something. We record it just in case we forget the tune.

The Helping Verb Song
(sung to the tune of "Jingle Bells")

Am, is, are

Was, were, be

Being, been, have, has

Shall, will, should, would

May, might, must, can, could.

We Learn with Songs

The Preposition Song
(sung to the tune of "Yankee Doodle")

About, above, across, after
Against, among, around, at
Before, behind, besides, between,
Beyond, by, down, like, during
Except, for, from, in, into, near
Of, off, on, over, past, through
Throughout, to, toward, under, until
Upon, within, without.

Bible Verses

My children have learned whole chapters
from the Bible by me putting tunes to the
verses.

Debi says

2¢   *"Singing works!"*

Absentee Dad

All seven of my children (now adults) are hard workers, have good attitudes, and seek the Lord. I have heard other military moms say they can't raise happy, hardworking kids because their husbands are not on board, but my children's dad was seldom home, as his job required him to be gone for long blocks of time, and only home a few weeks between. This is a list of things I did that I believe helped my family do so well.

We always worked together. Everything we did was as a team: cleaning the house, chopping wood, feeding the animals, homeschooling, or on the job, we were a team.

From an early age, I taught them how to control their own environment. They stripped their beds and remade them by the time they were five years old. They kept their rooms clean and orderly. I taught by helping them over and over until they had mastered the task. I was not their critic but their instructor. I taught them (including the boys) to cook full meals so they could be self-sufficient.

Music played a big part in their lives. It brought discipline, structure, and great enjoyment. We didn't have a TV, so music provided a lot of entertainment. I always had good quality music playing in our home and encouraged them to notice the harmony or the use of certain instruments. I am not blessed with musical talent, but I knew a family that thrived due to their singing together, so I used this tool. I made sure they had music lessons. I had a friend help us start a family band.

From an early age, I taught them to maintain self-control at all times. When they went to the doctor or dentist, they were allowed to cry if it hurt, but not to throw fits. Outbursts or out-of-control tantrums, fighting, and screaming were never tolerated. I did follow Michael Pearl's suggestions in his book, *To Train Up a Child*.

The greatest redeeming thing we did that molded my children was having jobs we could do together. We struggled as a team and we succeeded as a team. We had a paper route, sold cosmetics (the boys stuffed mailboxes with flyers), delivered phone books—any job I could get to make a little extra money and get the boys out learning how to make money. When they were a little older, I opened a fruit and vegetable co-op, and they helped. It taught them to respect other people, to put down any shyness, and approach everyone as a possible buyer, and it caused them to be thorough in cleaning, organizing, to buy good produce or other items, handle money wisely, and how to work fast. I paid them good wages and I deferred to their ideas of improving our business. I also paid my older children to watch the younger ones while the rest of us worked the co-op. I didn't use my kids. I respected their rights as individuals.

Often as the children were growing up, when my husband had been gone for months, I wondered if the children would fare better if I just divorced and raised them alone. But this one thing I am assured of…my children would not be the balanced adults that they are if I had taken that course. They respect the marriage vows as sacred. They see hardship as a thing to conquer not a thing that makes you miserable, and they appreciate the way they were raised.

I must say that, of course, after I read Debi's book, *Created to Be His Help Meet*, I could clearly see there were areas where I could have easily brought more harmony and peace to my marriage. Thankfully, I am still married to their dad, so I have begun to practice those principles. It has been hard to be a sweet wife after all these years, and it is hard for him to believe I am trying to please him; but he sees my effort, my true desire to honor him, and I can tell it pleases him. I always thought our strained relationship was due to the long separations and his over-dominance. I didn't see that I could have been training my children to honor him from afar. By faith I want to say that our marriage will one day be glorious. My grandchildren will see me honoring Pops. I am thankful for God's mercy.

from **Erin**

Since I was a little girl, I wanted to be an artist. I started drawing at a very early age and devoted most of my growing years with the study of art.

I realized there is art everywhere. Most people do not see it because they are not paying attention to all the details. God is our creator, the artist of everything that is. He made everything beautiful and good. Noticing all the beauty that he created causes you to appreciate the gift of art. God created our eyes to see and our hands to draw.

We only have to pick up our pencil and look, for without art and creativity, without all the beauty God creates, there is nothing.

"Art, like music, is more beautiful when expressing joy and gratitude."

Debi

Websites and Resources for Art found on pages 198-199

Crafty Ideas

Finger Paint

- 3 Tablespoons cornstarch
- 2 Tablespoons cold water
- ¾ cups boiling water
- Food coloring

Mix cornstarch and water. Pour boiling water into cornstarch mixture. Cool and divide into small groups before adding different food coloring. Doesn't store well so use liberally!

3D Maps

- 1 c. salt
- 1 c. flour
- 2/3 c. water
- Large map
- Tablecloth protector
- Wax paper
- Plastic knives or other shaping tools
- Paint varnish

In a large bowl, mix together salt and flour, slowly add water and mix until smooth. Knead dough until it is easy to handle. Place map on table, cover with clear tablecloth and then wax paper. Sculpt your dough map using the under map as a guide. Allow to dry for one week before painting and sealing with varnish. This recipe can be used for any project such as sculpting volcanoes, making mock Native American camps, or even creating letters and numbers.

Be a Turkey

Trace around the child's hand, color it like a turkey, and let them cut it out. Let them make a FLOCK of turkeys while you take a shower.

Painting Rocks

Kids love collecting rocks, but love to paint the rocks even more. They can pick whatever colors they want and sprinkle them with glitter for added fun. My kids will spend an entire afternoon painting rocks. When we go places, they pick up a couple special rocks to paint when they get home. It is like a memory rock. They have a whole collection of painted rocks and they always remember where they found them. It sparks an interesting conversation every time they bring out the rocks, and talk about all the adventures we had "that day."

Illustrating Stories

Every time my children write stories, I always have them illustrate them. They draw something they wrote about and color it. It is fun to look back years later at how a child communicates an idea. We all laughed when we found a story that Daddy wrote 30 years ago when he was their age. Keep their stories and one day they can share the gift of their story with their own children.

Fine Art Techniques
by Erin Harrison

Anyone can learn to draw or paint. It is a skill that can be developed through practice and patience. The most important thing I like to teach people is how to SEE. Most people will draw what they KNOW instead of what they actually SEE. (Eyes are shaped in many different ways, but most people draw the football shape because they KNOW that shape.) Basically, with all fine art, you must study the subject matter. It helps to touch the object and examine the angles and colors, the lights and darks. These are techniques for training a person to draw what they SEE—techniques for anyone who will dare to learn, from age 3 to 100 years old.

Blind Contour Drawing

This is done by placing a pencil through a plain sheet of paper. Have the child hold out the hand they do not use for drawing. The hand will be their subject. Tell the child to study the folds and creases of the hand. Next, place a blank sheet of paper under the paper with the pencil going through. The idea is that they can not see what they are drawing, hence the term "Blind Contour." They will begin drawing their hand, paying close attention to every detail. Make sure you tell them that their drawing is not meant to look good, it is meant to train their eyes. I am providing an example of a blind contour drawing I did to show how silly it will look if you do this technique correctly.

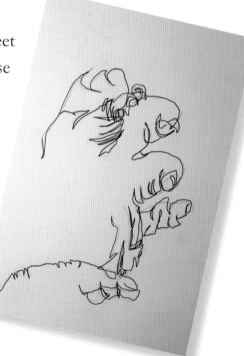

Still-Life Drawing

The next important technique is to set up a still life scene that can be drawn. Place a number of interesting items in the middle of the kitchen table, and have the children sit around the table, each with their own pencil and blank sheet of paper. Tell them that if they do not see the subject that is behind another object, they should not draw it. All of their drawings will look completely different because they are all seeing different things. Encourage the kids to look closely at the things they are drawing and notice if one object is half the size of the other object. If it is half-sized in real life, their picture should also show the difference. It really trains the kids to look at the spatial area of each object.

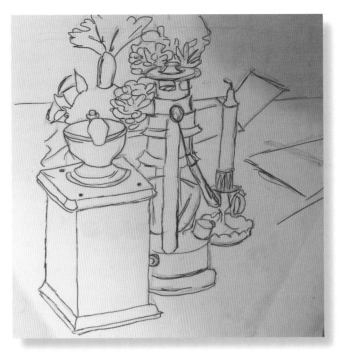

Here is an example of a still life drawing I did with my kids. We used various items found in the kitchen for this session. As you can see, some things are overlapping other things, I just simply drew what I could see from where I was seated.

Gradation Drawing

Another very important eye-training technique is gradation—the subtle differences between light areas and dark. In this excercise, no lines are allowed. You

can take an old brown paper bag and crinkle it up. Set it up on a table for all the kids to see. Give them each a pencil, eraser, and a sheet of white paper. They have to pay close attention to the detail in the crinkles. Remind the children how it is darker in the folds. Some areas are a lot darker where other areas are just a touch darker. This is the technique that will help them draw an object in a more three-dimentional looking space. A simple line drawing looks very flat.

Eraser Drawing

This trains the eye to SEE light and dark areas of the subject matter. Tape a piece of blank drawing paper to a hard surface. This will give a nice white edge when complete. Using a piece of black charcoal, "block in" the entire area of the paper so it looks like a black sheet of paper. With a paper towel, smudge the black charcoal to make a smooth black surface. Next, set up a few objects for a still-life scene. Concentrate on the light areas, and have the kids use an eraser to erase where they see lighter tones. The image will start to emerge, and the child will learn to see the subtle differences in lights and darks.

Understanding Color

To help your children understand color, they need to know that there are three primary colors from which all other variations of color can be made. The primary colors are: yellow, red, and blue. White is the absence of color and black is the saturation of all color. I have my kids make color wheels to train them in mixing and using color paints. On an old paper plate, squirt red, yellow, blue, and white paint in three different globs. Make a circle on a sheet of paper and have the children use the geometry skills they're learning to divide the circle into 12 equal parts. On the paper, block in a blue part, then count three spaces and block in yellow. Count three more spaces, and block in red. There should be space for three different colors in between the three primary colors. Next, they will take the yellow and add a very small amount of red to get yellow-orange. Add a little more red to get orange, and finally add a bit more red to get red-orange. After each color, add a dab of white to the pigment to see how that color looks in the light version (pastel colors). To make the green

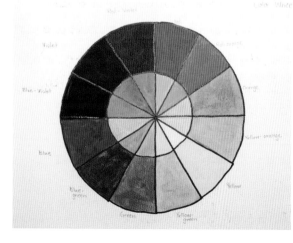

190

colors, mix a little blue into the yellow and block in that space as yellow-green. Add a bit more blue to get green, and finally add even more blue in to make a nice blue-green. Do the same with the red and blue colors to make three different variations of purple. This can be done using poster paint, acrylic, or watercolor paints.

Color Gradation

This technique will definitely help children understand how colors blend together to make subtle different hues. Taking a ruler, draw two 1x7-inch rectangles and one 5-inch regular triangle. (Use your geometry skills here!) Lastly, draw an irregular blob shape overlapping another irregular blob shape. For the first long rectangle, start with white paint in the bottom square. Have a child add just a faint amount of black for the second square. Each time they move up, add a bit more black, until you reach the final square, which is pure black. Start the next long 1x7-inch recangle with pure yellow and simply add a bit of grey each time until you get to solid grey. The same technique applies to the triangle. Start in the corners with red, yellow, and blue. Working your way to the middle, simply mix a little more color each time to get the very subtle changes until you get to the middle. The middle triangle is a combination of the colors from the three surrounding triangles. Finally, fill the blobs with orange and green pigments that the child has mixed. Where the pigments overlap, simply mix the two together to show what color is made by mixing them. This creates the illusion of transparency.

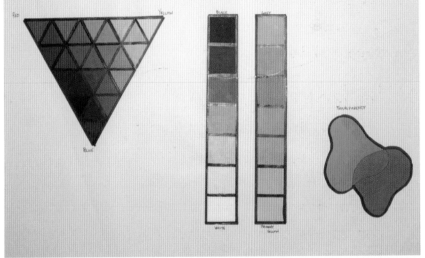

After having mastered some of these painting techniques, have them try painting a still-life scene!

Memories

Daddy and King Neb

Daddy's drooling and carpet-grazing depiction of "King Neb," changed into a beast, is so impressive that even three-year-old Joe is convinced of the value of being thankful and ascribing God the glory that is due Him.

As I pass by Joe and Rysha's bedroom every evening, I see their Daddy standing in the semi-darkness between the two twin beds. Sometimes he is crouched down like a prowling lion; other times he stands like a giant with a spear in his hand. Or, he can be seen kneeling with an arched back and hands upraised toward the sky. I see two little faces, eyes wide with wonder, peering out over the top of the covers. They've seen Daddy reenact so many Bible stories, you'd think they'd be tired of them. But the day isn't complete without the spectacular finale of Daddy's Bible story. And, I must confess, I sometimes hover in the darkness of the hallway, caught in the excitement of the story, and unable to go to bed until I hear the end.

The all-time favorite is about King Nebuchadnezzar, the greatest king on the earth since David and Solomon. God even told him so. But foolish Neb forgot who made him great, and took to himself the glory that belonged to God alone. Daddy's drooling and carpet-grazing depiction of King Neb, changed into a beast, is so impressive that even three-year-old Joe is convinced of the value of being thankful and ascribing to God the glory that is due Him.

The stories about Peter, Paul, John, and Luke in the Acts of the Apostles have started a regular occurrence of Joe standing on the back of the sofa with his arms outstretched, preaching to a wide-eyed Rysha (18 months old), who shouts unintelligible encouragement from her designated spot as his audience.

There is nothing somber or religious about "family devotions" in our house. Daddy's Bible stories have given our children a healthy appreciation for God's sense of humor, His justice, and His love. They know Him just as they know us—in a very real way.

I can't imagine "homeschooling" without that vital little hour at the end of every day. Teaching our children to read, write, and count to one hundred is minuscule in comparison to our desire that they come to know the Living God—their God! I rejoice to say that I believe we are succeeding!

"Drama is life with the dull bits cut out."

Alfred Hitchcock

 Websites and Resources for Drama found on pages 198-199

This is amazing. God told his people to be diligent in re-telling the Old Testament stories to their children and children's children because those stories introduced them to how God worked and why. They were the source of strength for the nation. These same Old Testament stories can be your family's strength.

Camera Hogs

When I had only three small bickering children, I stumbled on an idea that changed our lives. I pulled out the movie camera one day and caught them at their worst. Then I showed them in living color just how ugly it was when they fussed and fought. It did shock them, but they also started asking to make movies. Over the next few months, then years, we gradually gathered props for their camera adventures: wigs, outfits, staging, and other items including stuffed animals. I would read a Bible story (now we use *Good and Evil*) and then they decided who would be who. They studied their lines, practiced, and then dressed up. I rolled the camera. We got very imaginative telling stories like Lazarus being raised from the dead, the rich man in Hell, Moses, Samson and Delilah, the Last Supper, and so many more. We used a flashlight under the bed for dark drama. A single story would take them the whole afternoon to get ready for me to film. Sometimes I would just narrate the story and sometimes they created their lines. Over the years, we have covered an enormous amount of Scripture, and the children have a wealth of Bible history. They learned drama, camera work (which includes editing), memorization, and performing in front of others.

Now we have a huge library of dramas that they enjoy watching when we need a big laugh. It is fun to watch the children grow up in these films. All my children have grown to be gifted, disciplined actors and can, at will, become a different character. The bickering days ended with the entrance of the camera. My children caught a vision and it has carried through for years now.

The most remarkable thing is that now my young teens are paid very good money to film family gatherings, camp group meetings, preachers, and even weddings. After an event, my two oldest sit together behind the computer, with the younger children crowded around them, cutting, editing, and adding until the finished product looks and sounds like it came out of a very professional office. Occasionally they call me in to suggest some "old" music, but they have long since left me behind in abilities.

2¢ | *"Busy Mom... listen up!"*

Making Movies

With an inexpensive camera, I have moved into the movie business and we are the stars. Once a week, we set up movie school. The children put on their special clothes, which range from nice to really funny, and sit in the carefully arranged chairs ready to participate in Mommy's movie. With classical music playing softly in the background, I teach a math lesson using one of the children to help me hold the number cards. Then I have two of the other children come and hold word cards as I read through those; no repeats are necessary, for the movie viewed later is their repetition. Each session I try to have a new Bible verse song, read a poem, and share facts as well as math concepts. Each child is given an opportunity to be doing something smart as the film rolls. One silly face and that clip is cut out—and no one wants to be cut out, so this is usually a very notable work. After 30 minutes the movie is made. Using Photoshop, I add flash words, numbers, sentences, pictures, and whatever else I want to teach. It only takes me a few minutes to finish up the week's movie. Every morning, often several times each morning, the movie is watched by a very dedicated audience (younger children). If company comes over, they are compelled to watch the week's movie—and sometimes several weeks of school movies! The DVDs are carefully labeled as well as stored on a hard drive. You might think it is a lot of trouble for nothing, but that is NOT the case. All my children have learned to read with this method, although I only "taught" the lesson once. They all know the songs, poems, math, and Bible verses. When I need the small children entertained, it is so much better watching family school than dumb cartoons.

When you think about it, most of school is just repetition, which is what the movies do for me. It appears to me that learning is magnified by the act of watching yourself and your siblings as well as your mama teach. It certainly captivates them like no other movie does. They love "old" school movies better than anything. It cracks them up seeing themselves as "little kids" or else me nine months pregnant with them. Our movie making has proven quite successful in homeschooling my younger children, and now my older children are doing the editing for me, so even the computer work is passing on.

Several mamas have asked if I would make copies of our homeschooling DVDs for their children. How do you spell SUCCESS? My older kids want to start making them to sell.

○ ○ ○   No Greater Joy Ministries – Family Magazine, Child Training Art

◄ ►   ▲   +   🔒 nogreaterjoy.org

📖 ▦   **No Greater Joy**   **iMissionaries**   **Good and Evil**   **CreatedtobehisHelpmeet**   **Preparingto...hisHelpmeet**   `Bulk Hel`

No Greater Joy Ministries – Family Magazine, Child Training Articles, Marriage Resources, Bible Teaching Videos from...

Search   Websites and Resources

Websites and Resources for the Arts: Music, Art, and Drama

Music

- **Greg Howlett**

  Over 30 hours of instructional videos for church pianists. Greg Howlett is a Christian concert pianist, educator, and recording artist.

  http://www.greghowlett.com/about.aspx

- **Cornerstone Curriculum**

  Music can be a life-enriching, joyous experience. Even before your children begin the discipline of learning a musical instrument, make music be part of your home. The secret in developing a love for great music lies in enjoying it together.

  http://www.cornerstonecurriculum.com/Curriculum/Music/Music.htm

Art

- **Make Beliefs Comix**

  For the child who learns better when being creative, you might find this site helpful. Free customizable comics.

  http://www.makebeliefscomix.com/

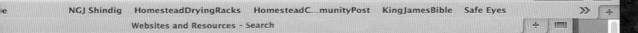

- **Art Made Easy**
  Many free art lessons to help you and your child start creating! New lessons added each month.
  http://www.art-made-easy.com/free-art-lessons.html

- **Make your own book**
  This site is one of my favorites for making school creative and fun. There are many fabulous books that you can make all by yourself. Let your imagination run wild with the simple, step-by-step instructions with illustrations to show you how to make some very creative and fun books!
  http://library.thinkquest.org/J001156/makingbooks/makeown.htm

- **Lapbook Lessons**
  Printable lapbooks, plus online photo and video tutorials that provides children with creative ways to learn.
  http://lapbooklessons.com/

Drama/Theatre

- **Play-Making: A Manual of Craftsmanship**
  by William Archer. Get the free eBook from this website.
  http://www.gutenberg.org/ebooks/10865

- **Patriotic Plays and Pageants for Young People**
  by Constance D'Arcy Mackay. Get the free eBook from this website: http://www.gutenberg.org/ebooks/18163

Gabriel's

Point Men of Action

Pearl Kid #2

Reflection upon ourselves and the world we live in is one human faculty that separates us from the animals. Having been created in the image of God, we intuitively know what is right and wrong. So I appeal to your own perception of truth. The pressures of this fast-paced world with our high standards of living and our big financial ambitions can distract us from the ultimate goal. A month turns into a year, a year into a decade, and our beautiful house will be left to our children, who will probably fight and squabble, and in the end they will go to court to see who will get the most.

On a five-day trip down through the Mexican Baja last year, my wife and I listened to some CDs on financial freedom. I'm usually not too big on the 1-2-3-step, Oprah or Dr. Phil plans, but this guy made some strong points that really hit home with us. Your first goal, if you are a child of God, is to love and respect your wife as Christ loved the church. Your second goal is to raise your children to be godly, upright people who in turn will raise godly children.

I'm trying to think of an eloquent way to put this, but I can't. So here it is: I see a lot of men whose jobs are more important to them than their families. Even the physical state of their home and their place in the community are more important. Very few would agree with me if I told them this. Some would get angry and tell me that I don't know their circumstances. Others would say that they are doing the best they can, but the proof is in their fruit, that is, in their children. Most men are more concerned for what their extended family and friends will think than they are about taking a radical step for their family's sake. They spent six years in school and are afraid to waste it by stepping off a ladder rung. When it comes to eternity, the number of steps you have climbed up the ladder won't matter at all. It's time for godly families to take charge, for fathers to step up to the plate, to quit waiting and to take action.

In the mid-70s, when my parents decided to homeschool, it was illegal in every state. Many men of God told my parents that it was wrong. Some families were very disappointed in them for taking this stand. How could my father, an ordained minister with a college degree, be so selfish as to deny his children the social and educational foundation that we children deserved, that only formal school could give? But my parents knew it was the right thing to do, and they did not back down.

So this is a call to action. If you are dissatisfied with where you are, and you are unable to spend the time with your children that you and they both deserve, then take charge. Stand up like a man. Know this: financial security is enormously overrated. The kids are better off eating cabbage and deer meat with you at the table than they are eating pop tarts alone. I am not suggesting that you should immediately quit your job and get radical. The point is this: if your children are getting eight hours of the world every day and only two hours of you, who do you think they will choose? The odds are stacked against you. Take thoughtful action.

My parents did, and their children are better for it.

—Gabriel Pearl

Shop
Class

"For a boy to learn to be a skillful craftsman,
he needs lots of opportunities to engage both his
body and mind with men's tools."

Debi

> "I make sure never to be negative toward my children while homeschooling. I want to make all learning pleasurable. I know this is my greatest tool. Here is some good hands-on learning."

Thrift Store Electronics & Tools

Broken radios, phones, TVs, and lawnmowers can be found either dirt cheap or as giveaways, and boys love taking things apart. Our ten-year-old son bought three lawnmowers for $2 apiece and used various parts from each to get one lawnmower running. He even used a spare part from one to "upgrade" his grandmother's mower before mowing her lawn.

Scrap Pile

My husband works construction and brings home random junk to add to a scrap pile behind the garage. One project I remember was when our sons made a chariot and used it behind one of our ponies. An old bicycle tire was made to function as the harness. Our only mistake was that we tried it out after dark with our pony that is blind in one eye. Easily adjusted…daylight is a real benefit.

Road Kill

While driving down the roads with my children, I have been known to allow them to throw road kill (that isn't too terribly stinky) into the back of the truck for further examination at home. We have scored a Great Horned Owl, porcupine, ring-tailed rat snake, squirrel, wild hog…I may be forgetting a few. I am sure we have a veterinarian in the making. If not a veterinarian, maybe a taxidermist.

(Debi says, "Be careful not to get a bad disease. Wear gloves, nose and mouth mask, and goggles.")

Daddy's Little Man
Shoshanna (Pearl) Easling

The other day, James decided to turn our old chicken coop into a creative playhouse where I can do my pottery. I am going to have a "sophisticated" arts and crafts center.

He installed three big, beautiful windows that we picked up at a yard sale, and then put on rustic metal and barn boards for the siding. Little Jeremiah James was as busy as a tumble bug keeping up with Daddy—learning to be a man. James would pick up the hammer, tack on one end of the board, put the hammer down, and in one swift movement Jeremiah would replace the hammer with a level—the next tool Daddy would need. He was very serious about his part. I wish you could have seen the glow on his face, knowing he was helping Daddy. Jeremiah was trying to think about what his daddy would need next. Sometimes James would reach out for the hammer, and his grinning son would hand him the level. Daddy would instruct him, "Jeremiah, bring the hammer back; I have to use the hammer to nail the siding on. I will use the level later." Even though Jeremiah had several tools available, he knew which one his daddy was asking for.

Photo by Laura Newman

Organizational Skills

It was interesting to watch Jeremiah James rearranging his daddy's box of neatly organized screws and nails. He put all the galvanized nails together, all the sheetrock screws together, and all the indoor nails in another spot. He did not notice size, so I showed him how to separate between type and size. Once he understood this concept, he immediately started to re-organize them back to their original arrangement. Just having an opportunity to handle these screws and get familiar with them was a learning experience that would prove useful the very next day.

Photo by Laura Newman

Building Confidence

Later that afternoon, James was busy with his chain saw, constructing a cedar pole trellis on the front porch of my Chicken Arts Center. As he cut the ends of the poles off, he would toss them a safe distance so Jeremiah could get to them. Jeremiah James decided that the cut ends belonged in the fire pit, which was some distance away and accessed by climbing up a steep eight-foot rise. It was fascinating that, without being told, he had elected to do a job that he felt needed to be done. Of course, we cheered him on. "You are so strong; good job, little man! Get another one." He continued working until James finished his project that evening. I have two men!

Self-Worth Because He Is Worth Something

The next day, when James was gone to work, I decided to work on our craft building. After getting a piece of metal siding up and in place, I realized I did not have my hammer and nails. Here I was, spread out, trying to hold up the metal and reach for the hammer at the same time. I really didn't think my small son would understand what I wanted, but I decided to give him a try, "Jeremiah James, can you get me a hammer and a nail?" Sure enough, here he came climbing through the small opening with the hammer and the nails. And not just any nails; he had the galvanized roofing nails. In a whole tray of various nails and screws, he remembered which ones I had used on the metal the day before. I am sure that his experience of separating the nails and screws played a part in being able to accomplish such a feat.

Every Minute Counts

Jeremiah is like a sponge soaking up every drop of what is going on around him. We have learned that whether you teach children something worth learning or not, they will be learning. It is a real shame when nothing but worthless nonsense fills their little brains, or worse yet, something really negative. I see children who are two and three years old who seem to not understand, when they are commanded to do something. They have learned to tune you out, unless it is a question concerning food, friends, going to town, or having a party. They have never learned to concentrate on a working command or project. It is foreign to them.

Training children is much more than, "Don't touch." Training is everything you do. They are watching and emulating, listening and experimenting, and constantly trying to figure out what you are doing so they can do it too. Little girls are learning

how to be wives. Little boys are learning how to be men. They remember what you did yesterday, and they will try doing it tomorrow. Scary, isn't it? It scares me into training my son to be the best of men.

Learning how to use the tape measure.

Shalom's Heart...
Daddy's Pride and Joy

Pearl Kid #4

When I was a little girl, I loved to be my daddy's "pride and joy." I remember Shoshanna and I would call Daddy to come and watch us ride our horses, see the play house we built, or watch us swing on a rope or vine. The best part of being his pride and joy was when we came into the house and Dad bragged about us to Mom. We always knew he was glad to be OUR daddy, and we knew he would not be as happy if we were not there to show him all of our great tricks.

I am now a mother of four, and I see my own children being their daddy's pride and joy. Just a few days ago, Daddy came home from work and the girls asked him if he would go to the creek with them and see what they could do. Even though it was fall, the evening was warm. It was almost dark as we all tromped off down the lane toward the swimming hole. Gracie, my seven-year-old, rode her 90cc Yamaha. Laila, the five-year-old, got the courage to ride her big sister's bike so Daddy could see that she could ride a big bike. Parker, our two-year-old, kept up a steady trot, running barefoot on the gravel. He stopped occasionally to pick up rocks but never stopped talking. I carried sleeping Roland in my arms. As we strolled, I thought, "Life doesn't get much better than this."

Gracie, being on a dirt bike, got to the creek before we did, so she made a big loop around the tree line before coming back toward us. That was when she ran over a small log, which made her struggle to maintain control of the bike. She succeeded in staying upright and continued to where we were. Her voice was shaky as she told her daddy what happened; she was trying hard not to cry. Seeing her distress, Daddy knew just what to do. He started praising her for not giving up and staying on her bike, continuing to ride to where we were. I reinforced what he was saying by telling her that she would be a stronger person because of that log in her way.

When we got to the swimming hole, the children all shouted, "Let's go swimming!" Soon the girls and Parker were each yelling louder and louder to get their daddy to see what they could do. Laila was swinging and dropping into the deep water, then swimming out again. Gracie wanted to show him how she could swing one-armed and do tricks on the rope. Parker, not wanting to be outdone by the girls, was swinging out over the creek and pulling his legs up and over his head, swinging upside down. Then he smiled with delight as his daddy clapped in praise. It was heavenly fun.

I have seen adults who are afraid to step out, afraid to fail, so they do not even try. They never were someone's pride and joy. Make sure your kids know that you are proud of them, even in the little things, so they will want to make you proud in the big things. Even now if you were to come by my parents' home, you might find any one of us five kids telling Big Papa (Dad) something we have accomplished. You know from reading his writing over the years that he still brags on us even though we are all grown with children of our own. It's my delight to pass his wonderful pride and joy secret to my children and, hopefully, now to yours.

208

Physical Education

"A sound body, as well as a sharp mind, requires action…lots of it."

Debi

Martial Arts

I enrolled the children in a Christian-run martial arts academy. I was looking for something that would teach the children a skill and give them an opportunity to interact with other children their age.

My youngest son is left-handed, and struggles with directions. Reading and writing were challenging for him. He also showed signs of dyslexia. He would write his name in the correct direction and then two minutes later write it again in the mirror image. After six months of martial arts, I realized that his reading and writing had improved by leaps and bounds! He was now consistently starting on the left side of the page! Another thing that it did for him, was helped him to stand on his own. Being the youngest, he could always rely on Mama or a bigger brother/sister to steer him in the right direction. Well, testing for a new belt meant he had to do his thing without looking to me for the answer.

Next, Child #4 is a rough-and-tumble kind of boy. Martial arts training has given him an outlet and helped him control his outbursts. During one sparring competition, he was getting frustrated and not doing well. I may have been the only one to see this, but he didn't lose his temper. He lost the round but maintained his cool; so in my eyes, he won.

Child #3 is a girl, and rather girly. Facing her brothers during sparring class has helped her be less sensitive to boyish teasing. She makes the sport look graceful. She has gained a degree of respect among her brothers, as they realize she is capable of kicking them in the head. Not that she would, but she could, and they know it.

On to Child #2. He's a skinny boy, all arms and legs. It's possible that the awkward teen years may pass him by, as he is working his arms and legs and getting them under control. He's 13 years old now, and has learned to push through new challenges and overcome. He has a natural tendency to shy away from anything that doesn't come easy. He has his eye on a black belt and is working through the physical and emotional challenges that come with each new level.

Our eldest daughter tried it for 6 months, and she said it just really wasn't her thing, so it is not for everyone. My children are better, stronger, more confident, and even more curious due to the training they have received this past year. The results are beyond my expectations.

Exercise Math

We take breaks for PE. While doing jumping-jacks, sit-ups, etc., we do math equations (1+1=2, 2+2=4), or we count by 2s, 3s, or do multiplication.

Marching to Music

On various pieces of paper, write down something you want your children to learn. For example, the alphabet, numbers, math problems, and history questions. Put one number on the reverse side of each page and lay the pages face down in a circle on the floor. Turn on the music and have the children march in circles, stepping on the pages. When the music stops, they pick up the paper they are standing on and read it out loud. If they are correct, the paper is placed on the couch and the music and marching resumes. When all the papers are off the floor, the session is over.

Tools for Keeping in Shape
by Erin Harrison

I wanted my children to become more active all year round. I found out that if I provide the tools and opportunities, the kids will keep in shape.

- **Summer –** We found an old canoe on Craigslist for $20 and hauled it to the nearest lake. The kids enjoy using their muscles to lift the canoe into the water and paddle. They love to jump in the water for a swim, which is wonderful exercise for them.
- **Fall –** We bought lots of balls at second hand stores. An old volleyball that the kids could bump back and forth, baseball and bats to practice hitting, basketballs to dribble, kickballs to play a game of kickball or foursquare, and soccer balls to kick around to each other. We looked up rules for each game on the internet and taught them the sport.
- **Winter –** We have cold winters and lots of snow, so we try to find cheap ice skates at junk stores. They spend hours on a flooded and frozen outfield in a local park playing broom ball or tag. They also have sleds to slide downhill with. On days that are too cold and blustery for playing outside, we make sure to have some ping pong balls and paddles so they can hit back and forth to each other. Sometimes we take the kids to the YMCA.

- **Spring –** When the weather starts to get warmer, the kids are looking for their bikes and balls again. They look forward to a hike in the woods or a family bike ride.

We try to have something fun and physical that they can do each day no matter what time of year it is. It keeps them in shape and gives them something fun to look forward to each day. The physical education becomes an incentive to get other schoolwork done so they can go out for play.

The Sunday Race
by Erin Harrison

Sundays are a day that many of our homeschooling families get together for fellowship. In the afternoon, families get excercise by doing various fun outdoor activities. It is exciting for the children to compete with other kids and especially their own parents. The activities include: volleyball, soccer, kickball, flag football, frisbee, and even racing. What fun to see families engage in training their own children with sporting activities that help keep everyone in shape. My kids love to see who will win the race each time, or who will make the best play in the game. It becomes a topic of discussion all week long. We encourage them to practice at home so they can one day win the race, too.

Shoshanna's Reflections

Pearl Kid #5

Healthy Broth

Old-fashioned broth is packed with important minerals that have disappeared from the American diet. They have been replaced with the discovery of monosodium glutamate (MSG). What is MSG? It is a neurotoxin that causes a wide range of reactions from temporary headaches to permanent brain damage. You might think you do not use MSG, but it is in bouillon cubes, canned broths and soups, dehydrated soup mixes, sauce mixes, TV dinners, most restaurant food, condiments, and more. It tricks the brain into thinking the food tastes better than it does. Fast food restaurants could not exist without MSG.

But enough about MSG; this article is about broth. So what is broth? It is a flavorful liquid resulting from slow cooking bones, hooves, egg shells, knuckles, chicken feet, meat, poultry, fish, or vegetables in water. This process pulls nutrients from cartilage and tendons, like sulphates and glucosamine, which is used as a supplement for treatment of arthritis and joint pain. Some of that stuff might sound a little disgusting, but believe it or not, it is delicious. The benefits for the body are amazing. It is an herb in itself, healing and strengthening the body's digestion. It contains minerals like calcium, magnesium, phosphorus, silicon, sulphur, gelatin, and trace minerals, in a form the body can easily absorb.

Broth has been used to treat arthritis and joint pain, peptic ulcers, tuberculosis, diabetes, muscle diseases, infectious diseases, jaundice, cancer, colds, and can even be put in babies' milk to aid digestion. Broth is also used to activate and strengthen the thyroid. Not only is broth great for your health, it is a MUST for culinary-minded individuals. I use broth for cooking vegetables, noodles, rice, sauces, soups, gravy, stews and more.

Health Class

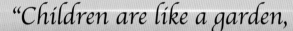

"Children are like a garden,

each a precious plant that will one day produce their
own unique fruit. Mom and Dad are the soil in which
they are planted. Homeschooling is the fertilizer
that makes them strong. The fun we have is the water
that keeps the plants healthy and disease-resistant.
Discipline and chastisement are the pruning that
cause them to bear more fruit.
We raise a garden, and we raise children."

Debi

Teeth

When my children brush their teeth, I sing to the tune of Ten Little Indians, "1, 2, 3-4-5, 6, 7, 8-9-10, 10, 9, 8-7-6, 5-4-3-2-1, SPIT!" Do this six times and you will get the recommended 2-minute brush, and your children will be able to count forward and backward at a very early age—while brushing their teeth. Once they can count to 10 in English I start singing it in Spanish.

Bath

We have discovered bathtub crayons! Phonics is fun, colorful, and very wet when learned in the bathtub. Our older children complain that we didn't teach them phonics in the tub!

Rub-a-tub

At bath time my children use bath crayons to write flash words, and any other word they remember. They also have a rubber measuring stick that they use to measure things. They each have a brush and cloth for cleaning the tub before they get out, so my tub is always pristine and clean.

Potty Training

I keep flash cards in the bathroom. When I go in to help my little one use the potty, I sit on the stool and show them two or three flash cards. I have a place where I can hang a new card each day. I don't know how it will work in the long run, as I only have two young children, but they enjoy learning while they are taught how to go potty.

Being Healthy
by Shoshanna (Pearl) Easling

Is your diet approach wrong? Dieting is usually not effective in the long run. Low-calorie diets will enable you to lose weight fast, but they will also almost always lower your metabolism. What's wrong with that? Lower metabolism means your food will not burn off as fast. Your body will be expecting less calorie intake because of the diet. Then as soon as you stop the diet, you will gain weight faster than ever before.

How can you lose it and keep it off? Clean your colon out. Try Detox+, cayenne, aloe, ginger, garlic, psyllium seed, and other cleansing herbs. Keep everything flushed daily. Drink lots of filtered water (or spring water) and take in fiber, flaxseed, chia seed, oat bran, rolled oats, whole grains, and whole wheat every day.

Get your liver and kidneys working right. If they function properly, your body can better process foods and eliminate waste. Look to milk thistle, burdock, dandelion root, fennel, bilberry, and of course plenty of clean water.

Photo by Laura Newman

Accelerate your metabolism with herbs and exercise. Get your heart pumping. Exercise at least three times a week, at least 30 minutes each time. After exercising, drink a big glass of an energy herb like green tea, ginseng, nettle, or all three mixed.

Curb your appetite. Feed your cells richly with vitamins and minerals; it is believed that these help to reduce cravings. Try nettle, fennel, bilberry, and chia seed. Taking a teaspoon of psyllium mixed well in seven ounces or more of water or juice 30 minutes before you eat will curb your appetite, making you eat less. It also helps regulate bowel movements.

Feed your cravings. If you know that you always start craving something sweet around a certain time, then plan on feeding that craving with something that will both satisfy and help you lose weight, like a cup of hot or cold herbal tea with honey and a dab of milk. Creamy and sweet! Try spiced chia tea, green tea, jasmine green tea, or Double E Immune Booster (one of my favorites, when taken with honey and milk). Carrots are pretty sweet too!

Eat whole foods high in fiber and lean protein like beans, whole grains, raw nuts, seeds, fruit, vegetables, wild game, and more. Stay away from processed foods. They are fat-makers. You are going to eat some processed food, but remember, even if it doesn't seem like a lot of food, it is fat food. Things like potato chips and cookies are highly processed and highly fattening.

You might ask, "Why do you recommend these herbs in particular?" Let me explain.

Bilberry is known to be an anti-aging herb. It helps purify the blood, promote healthy liver and kidney function, increase circulation to the brain, reduce inflammation and pain, relieve muscle spasms, strengthen blood vessels, improve night vision, and more.

Chia seed is one of the richest plant sources of omega-3 fatty acids. It is a rich source of protein, antioxidants, potassium, calcium, manganese, phosphorus, zinc, and copper, and it has six times more iron than spinach. Chia seeds are great in breads, granolas, and mixed into smoothies. Chia is great for your skin, blood sugar stability, endurance, and energy, plus it promotes healthy intestines.

Nettle is very high in many vitamins and minerals. From vitamin C to silica, nettle is one of the richest of herbs. It is also a wonderful diuretic that will purge your body of toxins while nourishing your cells. It is also believed to curb hunger.

Psyllium and flax help your colon regulate and flush out waste faster. Holding waste makes you gain weight. They can also be used to curb your hunger. Mixed in water or juice, they can expand up to five times in bulk. Flax is an excellent source of protein, fiber, and many vitamins. It stabilizes blood levels and strengthens the immune system.
~Shoshanna

Photo by Laura Newman

Nathan's Quest

Pearl Kid #3

Every night as I tuck my girls in and pray with them, I thank God for the things in my life. I thank him for loving me while I was yet a sinner. I thank God for dying for me, for giving me my precious children, money, health, and happiness. All this is good and important for them to hear, but that is not where they learn thankfulness. Those are big issues that are important to me, their daddy.

Financial well being is a difficult concept to grasp by the two-year-old mind. When I come home from work, hot, tired, and care-worn, and my wife greets me with a smile and a kiss, her eyes and spirit all say, "Thank you for what you've done for us today."

That is where my little girls learn a thankful heart. It is the spirit of the home that teaches thankfulness to my children, not just something that is said or taught. You can discipline for unthankfulness, but that does not create a thankful spirit. Thankfulness is a worldview. It is how you perceive your lot in life. Proverbs 23:7 says, "For as he thinketh in his heart, so is he." So, in closing, just in case you were wondering — YES! I am thankful that I have the best wife in the world.

Business

"If you want to build a ship,
don't drum up the men to gather wood, divide the work, and give orders. Instead, teach them to yearn for the vast and endless sea."

Antoine de Saint-Exupery

Just Write a Check

Several years ago, when my children wanted us to buy some item or to go out to eat, they started saying in a whiny tone, "Just write a check or charge it." They had no concept of banking or credit. My husband and I talked about the problem and decided to teach the concept by creating a banking system at home. The kids loved it. We set up a cabinet that had all kinds of goodies in it that the children could purchase. They received their banking credit, a card, and checks. We then explained to them how it all worked. The very first day, they went hog wild with purchasing. The next day, their bank was empty and their credit cards were overdue. They were given extra jobs to pay off the debt. The complainer went to jail, which was a chair in the corner, but he still was required to pay even if it meant tapping into his next week's pay.

Overall, the experiment was a great success. They never said, "Just write a check or charge it" again. All the children have matured to be very money-wise and have established their own side businesses.

Mom always gave us the open-book test because she said in real life you can always look the answer up.

Family Store

Each week, my children make a list of things for the family snack store. The things might include yogurt, cheese strips, chips, candy, cookies, or drinks. We discuss the list and I decide what to buy or not buy. Each child has to earn snack money by doing their chores and finishing their school work in a timely manner. Stars on a chart are added up and the total merits are listed. We have a chart with pictures of the different snacks and the merit amount beside it. A small bag of M&Ms costs 10 merits (almost no one wants to spend all their hard-earned merits at once, so they often split a bag), a cup of yogurt equals 5 merits, and an apple is free. Once the merits are spent there will be no snacks, except for the free ones. If a child doesn't spend their merits on a snack, they can "cash in" the leftovers for real money. Once the basic charts are made, this makes life a lot less complicated and stressful. Plus, it causes everyone to learn the wisdom of work, it causes a child to learn to exercise control in what and how much they eat, and it shows them how to save money. It also makes a way for chores and schoolwork to get done without any nagging from me. It is basically setting up a real-life work and reward system.

Vision

We decided that all our children would have their own businesses by the time they were teenagers. Our oldest daughter started her own egg business, keeping up with expenses by computer. We helped with the initial setting up of the chicken house and buying the first pullets. Her expenses included hiring her siblings to collect and wash the eggs, as well as the feed (eventually she started mixing her own with non-GMO, organic grain). The bookkeeping turned out to be her main interest. By age 10, she was actually helping Dad with Quickbooks, and now does the bookkeeping for his construction company.

My next child, a son, thought the animal business was for the birds, so he raised a garden and sold his produce. When he ran low on tomatoes, he had to buy from a farmer. The buying and reselling really was a hit, so he made contact with several gardeners, and thus was able to keep his vegetable stand going all summer and fall, raking in a very tidy windfall. This has become a regular summer endeavor. My next daughter read about Shoshanna's herb business, so she wants to do that next year when she turns thirteen; but who is to say she needs to wait?

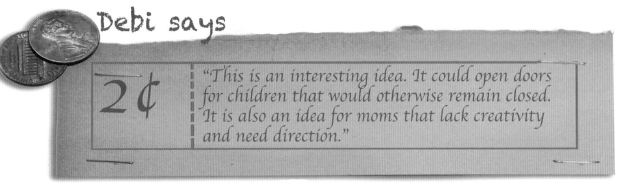

Debi says

2¢   "This is an interesting idea. It could open doors for children that would otherwise remain closed. It is also an idea for moms that lack creativity and need direction."

The Death Penalty and the Dig

Each of the last four years I have chosen three different professions to introduce to our children. I try to plan several projects around learning about these professions. We read several library books about what each professional does; if possible, I try to find a professional who will actually let us help them do their job. Last year, my children learned about preachers, electricians, and archeologists.

The Preacher

We read books on great preachers and missionaries and watched several missionary stories. We spent a day with our preacher, going to the hospital to visit, and then we helped clean up the church grounds. Each boy learned a verse of Scripture and quoted it at evening service.

The Electrician

Our study on electricity turned a bit morbid. First, we read how electricity was discovered. This really connected with both boys. One of my sons found a book about a dad who was electrocuted while wiring the family pool. I read it aloud to them. This led the boys to remembering that evil men were sometimes electrocuted by the state. They insisted we read a book on that subject. I found an electrician who was willing for them to walk through a house he was wiring, and he gave them a step-by-step of his job, including how dangerous it was. The man was a wonderful teacher and made a profound impact on my sons. Both boys came home wanting beginner's how-to books on electricity. We will do this profession again in three years when they are old enough to start planning for their futures.

The Archeologist

I didn't know an archeologist, so as part of a birthday surprise I planned a dig. A family in our church lives on a farm, and they said we could have a dig on their land. One day, I went out with a shovel and sack of bones I had saved from hams and chickens, as well as deer bones a hunter had saved for me. I planted all of the bones in a given area. My boys had already gone to the library for books on archeology, and while there, I checked out a simple book on common animal bones. On the way to the farm, we discussed what we might find on the farm at our dig and how the books say that archeologists make grids in order to document findings. We followed the rules; each boy had their tools and grid. The living animals had already found my ham and chicken bones, but the deer bones were a major success; with great skill they were properly cataloged, boxed and brought home.

This year my little girls are old enough to participate, which will make my job a little harder. For the next three chosen professions, we will learn about carpenters, artists, and lab technicians. Maybe next year we will learn about being a homeschool mom, a dad who drives a truck, and a grandpa and grandma who raise cows.

Passing Down the Graphics Trade
by Erin Harrison

I have been a graphic artist for about 10 years. Raising kids, keeping a home, and being a wife already kept me joyously busy, but I needed a creative outlet. When our children were really small I ran my own photography business while my husband did construction. When the business grew my husband started film work and we starting working together doing wedding photos and videos for clients, making a good income.

In the meanwhile, my husband and I had a desire to live out in the country. The kids were five years and younger, but old enough to work on our homestead helping care for animals, harvesting vegetables in the garden, and making dairy products from milk given by our family cow. We were living life in the country when we found our BIG vision. We were just beginners at the homesteading lifestyle, making our fair share of mistakes and learning from them as we grew together as a family. We thought, why not share our experiences with others? So the entire family became a team. What started as a plan to teach our kids how to live off the land while learning to be more responsible turned into the first film of the *Homesteading for Beginners* DVD series. We all took turns holding the video camera, teaching skills, and I finished up the project on the computer with some editing software.

Over the next six years, our family enjoyed making more homestead films together. The kids could share the skills they were learning with kids all over the world. In fact, we have gotten many very encouraging letters from families who felt by watching our family work together, it inspired their family to work together as well. What a blessing!

Besides working with my family, I am presently working with Debi Pearl on this homeschooling book as well as on other No Greater Joy graphics projects. My kids are getting to their teen years and it is time to pass down the computer skills I have acquired over the years. I am so glad that my kids will know how to survive by way of living off the land, or someday making a business for themselves doing graphics, film work, or photography.

This is my daughter, Megan (11 years old), learning how to use Adobe InDesign layout software.

Molly (13 years old), learning how to use Adobe Photoshop software for photo editing and graphic arts.

Miles (14 years old) at the No Greater Joy office, learning how to use the iMissionaries.org website along with social media to reach people around the world for the gospel.

Shalom's Heart...
Responsibility Train

Pearl Kid #4

My two-year-old son Parker loves to build trains. He has a big "Tom the Train" set, and he is always looking for someone to sit down and build a long track so he can push his train over the track while he makes chug-chug, choo-choo sounds.

I can remember when Parker first joined our family train as the caboose, just being pulled along behind the rest of us, enjoying the ride. It was obvious from the start, that he knew without him we would not be a whole train—that he was needed to make us complete. As he has grown older he has moved up in his responsibility, and it is a good thing, for soon a new caboose will take his place. Our "baby" boy has become a working train car.

When he was first learning to walk we would tell him, "Go close the door, Parker," and he would crawl or waddle over to the door, doing his job with pride. If one of the girls got to the door first, he would cry, for he knew it was his job, not theirs. He moved up in responsibility when he learned to take the garbage out for me, help carry the clean clothes, help wash dishes, and all the other things that let him know he was on the same track, pulling the same load as the rest of us. We are working together as a family to promote each child to a position in the train that is closer to the engine. Dad is the engine that keeps us moving forward, and we each have to do our jobs and follow behind.

This last summer Parker spent lots of time in the garden helping pick the tomatoes, corn, and beans, and then he would help can them. After we were finished canning, we carried them to the basement to be placed on shelves. He was a part of everything we did, for he is on the same track as we are, all going the same direction.

We go out as a family to cut wood for our fireplace. My husband cuts the wood while the kids and I pick it up and put it in the trailer. Parker works harder than the girls when it is outside, "boy work;" he loves to help his daddy. He will go for the biggest piece of wood just to show his daddy how strong he is. We back the trailer up to the porch to unload it. I stand on the trailer and the kids make a train that reaches from me in the trailer to their dad on the porch who does the stacking. They think it is the greatest fun in the world. If they were left alone to do the job, they would think it slave labor, but when we all work together, it is pure enjoyment.

A train goes nowhere without an engine and an engineer. Granted, the train moves much slower with all the extra cars. A two-year-old, four-year-old, and seven-year-old plus a round-bellied mama toting the next caboose are not very efficient, but thankfully we have a patient engineer (Daddy) pulling us along.

We cut some of the wood small enough that even Parker can carry it. It is his job to haul it into the house each day and stack it by the fireplace so Mama can put it on the fire to keep us warm and cook the beans that he so enjoys. He is quite happy being a part of the family train, and we are so happy to see him moving up in position. One day, he will be an engineer and command his own train with the confidence he gained little by little—the same way he gained responsibility.

Learning Styles

"To improve is to change; to be perfect is to change often."

Winston Churchill

 Great Books on Parenting found on pages 260-261

Websites and Resources for Learning Styles found on pages 262-263

Three-Week Courses

My children learn best when we all focus on one subject until we complete it. We study science and history like this as well as other subjects. My older children love to open up a science book and know they can work on it until it is complete, so sometimes we all study a science book for three weeks. The older children learn along with the younger as they help them read about science. I learn as I read along with my older children. We do science experiments together, go out hunting earthy things, and grow slime and all the other weird things that go along with science. On camera, each child finishes up with a summary of what they learned.

Equine Studies

I am a "letter of the law" mama. I have always followed curriculum page by page as if it were the Bible, and have thought poorly of those that did not. I called all other types of school "silly distractions." Then I had a visionary daughter: obedient, kind, loving, and willing to obey, but very far behind in her ability to study and learn. It alarmed me that for blocks of time she seemed almost sad. She kept saying she really wanted to be a horse whisperer. After reading the NGJ magazine, I knew I had to allow her to do school her way. So, in the place of her regular school books, she began watching and reading everything on training horses. She worked to save money so she could pay for horse riding classes. She more than excelled. Within the year she was teaching volunteer classes. People, both children and adults, began to pay her for private lessons. Her clientele grew. Now her interest has moved into equine nutrition, massage, and medicine. When she is not riding or teaching, she is studying. The once poor reader now pores over medical books like they were a teen magazine (which she deplores). And yes, the once sad, defeated child now talks with great confidence and has an endless stream of ideas for her future. I often wonder what would have become of my different child had I pressed her into my "dead works" mold. I am so glad I listened to my heart.

Debi says

2¢ *"I love this! This child was allowed to follow her own vision."*

Schooling That Works

Do some of your children hate school? If so, it is probably because what is being taught does not translate into real life. Learning something new should spark creative thinking. It should stimulate the mind to ask why, what, how, or when. Learning is like tasty, nourishing food for the brain; the body simply craves, needs, expects, and lives by good quality knowledge. There is no joy or satisfaction apart from personal growth and fulfilling the yearning to know. God instilled in us the drive to learn, excel, and use that know-how to help others. If your children hate to learn, then they are either learning the wrong thing or it is taught the wrong way, and the results will be poor both in the mind and in the soul. Stop, dump your curriculum, and start afresh. This time, remember the end result is to instill a love for learning. The pursuit of knowledge and wisdom is best gained when there are hopes and dreams and a struggle to overcome. Our children should be constantly stimulated with possibilities. A child performs best when focused and committed.

Example for a Very Young Child

A daily focus could be learning about one particular animal and then preparing to share that information with the family. The whole day of learning should be woven together around that animal: art, math—an example would be counting the days of gestation using a calendar, or counting the number of babies carried—reading, language, writing, and studying YouTube videos about the animal. Then, at the end of the day the child learns the rewards of how to share his knowledge with others.

Today, my grandson ate his first fig picked from the tree. As he was eating the fig, he noticed how sweet it was and wondered what percentage of sugar was in a fresh fig. Because his mind was already stirred by the fig, we changed our day's homeschool plan over to the study of figs. We "Googled" figs and read about how to plant them, where they grow, how to get more fruit from each tree by breaking off foliage, and how to preserve or cook with figs. After several hardy discussions, we studied the nutritional quality of figs. We both learned, and when his mama came in the door he announced to her that the fig was the most nutritious of all fruits.

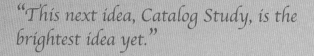

"This next idea, Catalog Study, is the brightest idea yet."

Catalog Study

My best homeschooling tool is catalogs. Yes, junk mail. Only for us, most of our catalogs are not junk. I set about to get on mailing lists that are productive—catalogs selling every sort of animal, such as chickens, ducks, cows, goats, birds, and also the supplies to care for them. We get catalogs that feature vet supplies, seeds or plants, herbs, worms, hunting and fishing supplies, bird houses, trees, and bees. There are also all the electronic catalogs that keep us busy and abreast of the latest and best of everything. Once your name gets on a list, they sell your name to other such catalogs, so we get a bunch. We do most of our buying through catalogs (I don't order dress catalogs, and if a nasty catalog starts coming, I nip it in the bud with a call).

The diversity of the catalogs makes them a readily available teaching resource and a wonderful wish list. Questionable pages are easily ripped out before they are passed out to the general family population. You would be amazed at how much you learn by studying these catalogs and how much the children learn by making an order. For instance, once it is determined that we want to buy quality non-GMO seeds, out come the catalogs and we search for the best deal. Several of the children might take a catalog each and figure the same order. This allows us to see which catalog gives the best deal. Often we end up ordering our plants from one catalog and seeds from another, but then we determine if the shipping makes that an extra expense or a better deal. If we start getting a magazine that is not of our standard, I have one of the children call the toll-free number and request to be taken off the list.

My children have become familiar with so many products that when we do go to a store they are quite capable of knowing the true value of any given product and the quality at a glance. It gives them confidence to be able to discuss with professionals the quality of feed for this animal or the medication required. They can step into a camera shop or computer store and speak with the people as if they owned the store. So reading, writing, math, science, health, history, etc., are all learned in catalogs. Yes, we use catalogs—free junk mail—to become proficient at any number of professions. It really works.

Teacher for the Day

On Fridays, the children take turns being the teacher, and I take their place as the student. They have to teach me their work and help me understand it. They have to grade my work and they KNOW I always make sure to leave mistakes, so they have to be sharp and grade correctly. They LOVE being my teacher. My other children love to watch their siblings teach Mama school. I think they learn more on their Friday as a teacher than they do any other day of the week. It brings out the leader in them as well.

Taking a Friend Along

My young niece sent us a 20-inch cut-out picture of herself glued to cardboard and asked us to take her everywhere we went on our vacation, and to make sure to include her in as many of the family pictures as possible. Our girls loved having Flat Fran along for the ride, and taking pictures was so much fun. When we emailed the pictures to her, my girls called her and talked about each picture, telling her in detail everything of interest. As I listened, I realized how much more they learned from their travels, knowing they would be telling someone they loved about each place and event. Geography, history, culinary experiences, horse shows, and other areas of learning were all engrained in their minds, thanks to Flat Fran.

An Adoring Fan

From the beginning I started sending my son's best papers to his Grandma. Now he wants to print her address on the envelopes and fold his own papers. We only visit her once a month, but when we do she holds him tight and tells him how wonderful his letters are. I am sure he will outgrow the joy of pleasing his Grandma, but at 7 years old it makes him a much better student.

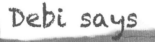

Debi says

2¢ *A smart mama with teens will read the next letter and ask herself, "How can I find a place for my teens to serve others?"*

Help Cometh

Big Heart Award

My youngest, Little Guy, is special needs. His therapy requires four hours of stretching and bending (broken up into several sessions). Trying to homeschool my other children as well as keeping up with housework, cooking, keeping the fire going in our old stove, and a thousand other chores was just too much.

Reluctantly, I went to a homeschool support meeting and asked for volunteers. God gave us a miracle. Now Little Guy has several Handmaiden Mommies helping him with his therapy, reading to him (his greatest delight), and also helping me with homeschooling my other children (they LOVE having the girls do school with them). I weep as I write this. I weep with joy. Our five Handmaiden Mommies range from 13 to 24. They are homeschooled girls, willing to weekly give of their time for us. Each girl is so gracious, acting as if we are blessing them for providing the opportunity to be of help. Every evening my children pray, asking God's special blessing on each of our Handmaiden Mommies. This is one request I know God will richly bestow.

Debi says

"Most children do better if there is some consistency in their lives. Sleep schedules, blankets, cups, same place for schoolwork, etc. They like to know what to expect."

Vision Creativity begins with imagination; conceiving a thing that is not but should be, and then taking steps to make it reality. It is facing a problem and envisioning an original way to solve it satisfactorily.

What is Creativity and Is It Important?

Creativity can be born of practical necessity or artistic expression, but it is original to the individual—not done before, or not done in the same way. Without creativity there would be no innovation, no progress, nothing new or different. Think of the tools and trades that never would have existed without creative thought. Man would remain very primitive—no houses, cars, computers, planes, or even artificial light. Disease would have no cure. There would be no beautiful music or art.

God is creative. We are the proof of that. Being in his image, it is our nature to create—to endlessly strive to come up with something that amazes and gratifies. Creativity is associated with happiness and success in life. Creative people are interesting people; the lack thereof makes one a wallflower. Just a few years ago, operational efficiency was the yardstick of market success; today it is all about anticipating consumer demands. This translates into the insight to conceive of a heretofore-unknown product that meets a need, or at least a new way to market an old product.

Is Creativity an Inborn Gift?

Why are some people creative and others not so much? I have often heard people say, "Oh, I just wasn't born with the gift for creativity. I am better with numbers and facts." This statement simply is not true. Researchers have found environment to be more important than heredity in influencing creativity, and a child's creativity can be either strongly encouraged or discouraged by early experiences in life and in school—including homeschool.

Are Your Children Creative?

Ask a group of eight-year-olds if they are creative and 95% of them will say, "Yes." Ask twelve-year-olds and only 50% will say, "Yes." By the time students finish school, only 5% will say they are creative. The fact is, we are all born with creativity but it is pulled, wrenched, strangled, pried, screamed, and bored out of us by the time we are adults. Creativity can't be tested, so it has generally been abandoned. Yet now, by questioning large numbers of successful people, it has become apparent that creativity is the key to their success.

Homeschooling began as a creative explosion that was pulling children from the ranks of sameness and giving them a vision of all that is possible. Then came homeschool curriculum—same-old, one-cover-fits-all books and tests. Then quietly, the homeschooler began to fall back into the line of uniformity. What a crying shame!

How Can We Unleash Creativity?

Every child is born to be an artist, a storyteller, an inventor, and an explorer. Expanding creativity in children takes place when we turn them loose and teach them to have grit, determination, perseverance, and belief in what they are doing. Adults have a tendency to want to see the end of a thing; but creativity comes in bits and pieces. A creative person rarely sees the whole, only the piece he is touching at any given moment. Creativity can't be hurried. Anything rushed is just a stamped-out repeat, and is not part of the creative experience.

Many years ago, when I was in

school, my art teacher made a dumb mistake in a class full of gifted artists. She gave each of us three pieces of colored paper and told us to create a picture using those papers. She wanted us to be creative, but the idea she had in her head was just that— in her head. The three-colored project was a boring, frustrating experiment for the whole class. If the teacher had been wise, she would have shown us two or three examples of how an advertising company used three colors, and in doing so would have unleashed a ton of creativity. The most powerful way to develop creativity in your children is by example—your example and the examples of what other people have done.

Hurry and creativity cannot sit in the same seat.

There is real pleasure in creativity. Controlled studies have shown that children who are allowed to be creative associate joy with making something new. Sometimes all a child needs to get started on a project is a good question. Instead of making a suggestion, ask a question: "Does this blue remind you of sky, water, or a pretty dress?"

You might notice a child staring at a pattern on the kitchen wallpaper, so you ask, "Do you see something? I think I see an alligator in that pattern."

Homeschooling mamas are almost always in a hurry. Hurry and creativity cannot sit in the same seat. Stationing a baby or toddler in a splash of warm sunshine pouring through a window where he can stack blocks, paper, and various objects, is a simple, soothing, creative afternoon activity. Letting children play in the dirt, making roads, bridges, lakes, and buildings is creating the next generation of builders and makers. Sitting them in front of electronic media, even educational media, is killing their genius and squashing creativity. Sitting them down with a stack of workbooks that bore them silly is creating silly kids. Consider this: Any project that they get involved in—whether it be music, painting, mud building, writing, storytelling, stacking, making tents, performing plays, making cameras, or whatever—should result in someone being able to say, "Wow, that is interesting. What are you going to do next?"

Old School, New School

As children mature, creativity will begin to involve long-term projects. Songs that need hours of careful trial-and-error, poems, stories, articles, term papers, research, and building projects can lead to frustration or despair without patient perseverance. Encouraging a budding mind to persevere is critical. An important lesson in life that will be reflected in all areas of maturity and godliness is learning that life is work, and that rewards for greatness only come with time and energy. You don't immediately become an expert musician, artist, writer, or builder. Good things come to those who stick with it. This lesson could be called discipline, learning to harness your feelings and drives for the sake of long-term accomplishments.

Schoolbooks are set up for short-term accomplishment. "Finish your pages and then you will be through," I have heard said a hundred times. The end of today's torment is near…yeah! This type of schooling does little to teach children the value of delaying gratification. School projects are a much better way of teaching, and they are certainly more conducive to developing good character.

In today's society, knowing how to research is a thousand times better than knowing facts. Information is now at our fingertips. We live in a different world than we did 25 years ago, yet homeschooling curriculums are developed in the old world of knowledge. Once, schools were the gatekeepers of knowledge, and memorization was the key to success. We tested a child's ability to regurgitate facts and formulas. That day is over. Yet even in the old-school program, children came home each evening to run and play, chase the wind, and build doghouses. There were hours of creativity that children don't experience today due to electronics.

I would that all children became tinkerers and thinkers. If we are to remain a free, strong, and confident people, then this next generation needs to dream, create, work hard to make it happen, and then take the next risk.

Questions to Ask

- Are you homeschooling your child in a way that cultivates creativity, or stifles it?
- Is your household structured to encourage creativity?
- Are you so regimented in finishing school books that you leave no place for developing creativity?
- Are you conditioning your children to lead a dull life, not becoming accomplished in business?

Facts to Consider

- From the perspective of CEOs, creativity is now the most-valued quality in a potential employee. In an IBM research study, about 60% of the CEOs polled cited creativity as the most important leadership quality.
- In the world of business, studies prove there is a strong connection between trust, character, and creativity. Trust in a company, a family, and even in a government, unleashes creativity. The knowledge that we are all working to make a better life for everyone causes an individual to reach for greater ways to serve others. This environment of goodwill allows followers to take risk. Risk is associated with creativity. Where there is no scary risk, there is no creativity.
- Creative individuals are naturally more unafraid of experimenting with new things. They think more about ideas and less about what people think of them, thus they are often less susceptible to peer pressure. Studies show creative people tend to be self-reliant and willing to go against conventional "wisdom."

Creativity Killers

- Don't patronize children by offering rewards for their creative labor; it will steal their pleasure.
- Be careful not to make your child a nervous wreck by unconsciously setting up expectations of grandeur. Be practical in your expectations, and let his vision of what he can do grow with his abilities.
- When your children are involved in creativity, don't hover over them or instruct them on how to improve their creations.

- If your child is making something, don't feel compelled to evaluate his project.

- So you're an adult and can show your child how to do it better—don't. Let him have the joy of discovery. It is much more valuable than the outcome.

- Please don't set up creative projects that suit your house-cleaning habits. Take the kids to the library and turn them loose on ideas. You might sit on the floor and look through "how-to" books with them. Let them come up with ideas they would like to try. You can coach, but don't poach.

Wonderful Birthday Gifts for Brilliant & Creative Homeschool Kids

1. A chicken (live)
2. A bag of cement
3. A big load of sand
4. A shovel
5. A hay-bale house (bales to build their own)
6. A fruit tree
7. Homemade play-dough (let them make)
8. A flashlight
9. A pocket knife
10. A retractable tape measure
11. An old typewriter
12. Any kind of nuts in the shell and a cracker
13. A fishing trip
14. A baby brother or sister
15. Old paint and brushes

Creativity
by Rebekah (Pearl) Anast

The Teacher

Boredom was an unknown ailment in our house, thanks to Mom. With the energy of ten monkeys on NoDoz® pills, she started one project after another and completed at least half of them. Her curiosity was and still is insatiable.

I remember her standing over a boiling cauldron of black walnut hulls, hands and bare feet stained dark brown. She was making dye. Not because she needed it, but because she wanted to know how dye was made. Library books stood in shifting stacks on the kitchen table, ranging in subjects from herbal concoctions used in China, to crochet stitches known only by people over 95. She taught us to question, to wonder why and how about everything. How does a caterpillar change into a butterfly? Put it in a lunch box with leaves, and watch! How does a potter's wheel work? Get a book, and follow the directions. What does oatmeal do to your face? Put it on and let it dry, and you'll find out. Mom wasn't afraid of trying anything.

I was born with dyslexia. I saw everything as though I were looking in a mirror. School had not been an easy thing for Mom either. She is deaf in one ear and partially deaf in the other, but she was undaunted at the prospect of teaching me how to read. She brought home all the research she could get her hands on and set out to experiment on me. We drew in the sand with our fingers; we did finger painting and shaped letters with play-dough; we made our own play-dough with peanut butter, powdered milk, and honey, and ate it when lessons were over. We read *Matt the Rat* over and over and over until I had it memorized. I was only four years old at the time. I had lots of fun and had no idea I was "in school." By the time I was six years old, Mom had "retrained" my brain. I have very little manifestation of dyslexia left. I read and write voraciously, thanks to Mom's creativity. I'm so glad she didn't just shrug in hopeless sorrow and send me off in the short, yellow bus to special education classes in public school! I might still be there.

The Curriculum

I never knew Mom to spend much money on curriculum. She always looked for old school books at secondhand stores and garage sales. It's amazing what up-to-date curriculum you can find in those places. However, to tell the truth, we did very little bookwork. Less than you would believe! Instead, we counted out the change in our five-gallon penny-bank, and had spelling contests, drawing contests, and wrestling contests regularly. Dad told us historical stories at the dinner table and quizzed us on previous "lessons." In the woodshop, we learned to read a tape measure and figure angles and planes. In the kitchen, we learned measurements and a bit of chemistry. In the garden, we learned the difference between a bushel, a peck, and a five-gallon bucket. And last, but not least, in the creek we learned the reward of faithful labor!

Learning was a way of life for us.

Learning was a way of life for us. Occasionally, in the dead of winter, during a cold spell, we would have two or three weeks of intense bookwork and lessons. Every one of us would progress a grade during that time. Not because we learned that fast, but because the rest of year was filled with the practical aspects that the bookwork only talked about. Each one of us had weaknesses and strengths. I loved to read. Gabriel loved math. Nathan loved science. Shalom loved medicine. Shoshanna loved art and music. Mom allowed us to pursue and excel in whatever area we were good at. Whenever I got bogged down in math, Dad would sit down at the table and teach us a math lesson. Whenever the boys got frustrated with reading, Mom would read halfway through a Louis L'Amour book aloud and let them finish it.

I think in many ways, homeschooling was easier for Mom than it is for many of you out there, simply because Mom started back in 1977 when there was "no way to homeschool." Even A Beka Books wouldn't sell curriculum to homeschoolers back then, so Mom had to be creative. There was no homeschool group in our town to compare ourselves by. We were it. There were no homeschool magazines or books and no support groups. Now that I'm grown and homeschooling my own children, I'm glad my Mom had to be creative. Her slapstick way of doing things has given me freedom as a mother to use what I need of "traditional" homeschooling, and let the rest go. My children's love for learning is my first concern, and learning will last a lifetime if creativity is at the heart of it.

He that has ears to hear, let him hear...

Know Your Child

Yesterday I had a wonderful day with my seven-year-old son. I drove two hours to drop off my other children with my parents for their once-a-month night over. Usually their stay-over coincides with a time when their truck-driving daddy is home, which allows us to have a monthly date night. This time was different; Dad was on the road. I had never done this before, but I had noticed my son seemed to be getting distant, short-tempered, and he had come to hate homeschool. His growing bad attitude set off my alarms. When we got back in our town, we went straight to the library for books that I could read to him that evening. The books he chose were not what I would have selected, but somehow I knew this was not about learning facts but rather tying strings of fellowship. I smiled and told him they looked like fun. We stopped by the grocery store where we went in together and bought fried chicken and biscuits, which we took to the park to eat. Afterward, we played on the swings and slides and just chased each other around laughing until it was almost dark. Even though it was evening by the time we got home, we did his school paces together. He really loved working one-on-

one, and it went quickly because he had the benefit of my undivided attention and I was able to answer most of his questions. I thought to myself, "Why haven't I tried this style of schooling before?" It was so productive and fast. Then we sat together in the big chair and read all the library books he had picked out earlier in the day. He said he wished he had checked out a hundred. Again, I was surprised at his interest and questions. Had I been stifling his mind with my nit-picking, do-all-your-page-or-else attitude? At bedtime, I lay beside him and told stories of when he was a little guy, then stories of when I was a child. Somewhere along the evening he started talking. He told me everything he could think of and some of it twice. I really came to know my son as a human being in those brief minutes; he wasn't just my baby, or even my son, he was an individual who had ideas and dreams. Finally we prayed together and I climbed over into the other twin bed. I heard his long, contended sigh, and then he said, "This is the best day I ever had. Thank you, Mama." I have to say that I silently cried. I am an event planner and organizer. I count minutes and like things clean. So many times I have taken my children to this exciting activity, or that great learning event, or even out to a fine dinner, but just to spend the time being a one-on-one mama had escaped me; maybe, being a mama had almost escaped me. Thank God for second chances. So, yeah, this is my best homeschool idea.

The Roland Study
by Debi Pearl

My grandson Roland, who just turned one year old, has taught me more about the development of babies and toddlers than I learned my first sixty-plus years of life. It is not that he is such a fine teacher; it's just that now I'm a grandmother, and not responsible for meeting the daily needs of my children. Now I can seriously focus on what makes him tick, how much he understands, what causes him joy or anxiety or fear, his interests and responses—and, most importantly, what a child is capable of learning at various ages.

When he was just a few months old I began "studying" him in great earnest. I had the feeling that I was quietly listening to him speak before he could actually talk. I learned that either this little guy is a remarkable kid or all of us big folk are missing the budding intellectual life of our small babies.

Are babies frustrated by their baby bodies? Before Roland could sit up, it was apparent that he was intently studying his siblings in their play. His body language spoke volumes. His muscles tensed when they laughed, and he waved his hands and kicked his feet when they all ran outside. He yelled wildly when the other children came back inside after playing. And—the most robust reaction—when his siblings started saying that Daddy was coming home, Roland would really get wound up.

As I observed his different responses, I could clearly see that he knew what was happening and wished he could join the parade of feet running here and there. This baby boy was frustrated by his baby body. What can a baby learn, and would he be more satisfied if we were engaging him in learning?

I have observed him not so much as a grandmother, but more as a researcher with keen interest in how much a baby can know or learn. I have been trying to understand early development for almost 40 years since my oldest child was a baby. At that time I read everything I could find on the subject—including opposing viewpoints. *Better Late Than Early* by Raymond and Dorothy Moore is right on. I also read two books by Glen and Janet Doman, *How to Teach a Baby How to Read* and *How to Teach Your Baby Math*. The Moores advocated waiting to start any schooling, and the Domans said to start teaching at birth. So which one wins—early or late? Dr. and Mrs. Moore's writings were from the psychological perspective about structure and how it squashes a child's natural curiosity. At the time Moore wrote, all early education was understood to be in a formal, structured, classroom sense. The resounding failure of the Head Start program proves that what they wrote was dead-on.

I learned that our goals should be creativity, wisdom, curiosity, investigation and understanding.

The Domans wrote on how much a child's mind can pick up if that information is just part of his daily life—with no stress, no structure, and no challenges, just opportunities to learn something. When I read those books, and others, I was galvanized. As a young mother I was ever ready to experiment, so I followed their instructions by making word cards, softly playing high-quality music to my newborn (24/7), and reading poetry to her as I nursed. Since I didn't have another child to compare her progress with, I just assumed she was learning on par with other children.

At the time, my measure of success would simply have been academic skills, which are almost meaningless to me now. I have learned that our goals should be creativity, wisdom, curiosity, investigation, and understanding. Facts are meaningless unless they have context. But for my firstborn, the experiment worked. Even at a

young age, she was a poet, loved music, and was an avid story writer, all of which serve her well in her adult life. She acquired knowledge, but more importantly she came to love the process of learning; she became a student of people and an observer of the world around her.

As I had more children, I taught them in the same manner, achieving the same positive results. Though what I had learned about early training had lost its luster, a very important concept had firmly taken root in my mind: the habit of expecting my babies to find pleasure and understanding in my daily activities, whether sweeping the floor or hunting for a rare herb in the woods. My children grew up sharing every good idea that came into my head. They were partners in investigation and creation. Instead of thinking silently, I talked to them about what was going on in my mind, because I wanted them to know and love the wonderful things that I found so stimulating.

At the time I read the Domans' books, homeschooling was a new concept, and almost everyone, including my family and friends, thought the very idea of homeschooling was insane and would produce social misfits and morons. To add to that, there were plenty of pessimistic people ready to tell me that it was silly to waste my time showing word cards to my babies, and "it would surely cause them to have emotional issues." I was told that I should just enjoy my babies and (spoken silently) keep them dumb. (On a side note: Would you believe that in the early 1970s, breastfeeding your baby was frowned upon by doctors and nurses? A registered nurse told me that nursing a baby "with your breast" was vulgar, and no good Christian mama would ever do such a thing.)

Back to homeschooling: Many years have passed and now my firstborn is a middle-aged lady—very musical, my only child who can spell any word, an amazing writer, and forgive me, just brilliant!

Back to Roland: As I was studying my grandbaby, I kept asking myself, "What can a baby learn, and would he be more satisfied if we were engaging him in learning? And if we used that first year to the fullest, would it change the rest of his life, making future learning easier? Would early learning build a strong foundation?" You have to live an entire lifetime to be able to answer these questions—one of the perks of being old. So, based on homeschooling my five children for twenty-plus years and now watching my 21 (and still counting) grandchildren being homeschooled, plus having read hundreds of books on various subjects pertaining to these concepts, and after observing Roland, I now feel that I can be definitive.

Q & A

Q: What can a baby learn?
A: A lot more than we are capable of understanding.

Q: Would babies be more satisfied if we were engaging them in extensive learning?
A: It has proved so in my experience.

Q: Would it change the rest of their lives if we did engage them in learning?
A: Yes. I believe that infant learning creates a foundation that causes children of average intelligence to flourish in life, to become confident leaders and innovators.

Q: How can I do this?
A: It's easy...just treat your baby like he or she has brains and can learn. Always assume that your cranky baby is sleepy, sick, or bored, and do something to alleviate the problem or meet the need.

I want to get back to my study of Roland. On the first day that he could walk just a few steps (about nine months of age), he made his way to the laundry room. Without a moment's hesitation, he plopped down and grabbed the broom, nearly knocking his head. The loud bam as the broom hit the floor caused him to jump and pucker up for a cry, but not feeling harm he continued his adventure. I must say, Grandma was sweating. The older I get, the more nervous I am about all the little "ouchies." But I kept myself in check and observed without interruption. Roland never missed a step. He grabbed the head of the broom, stuck it between his legs as leverage, and began to turn the handle around and around, unscrewing it from the broom. It took a lot of grunting and effort, but he managed to get the handle separated from the broom. When the sweeper came off into his hands, he squealed with triumph, and held it up for me to see. I was amazed. Three months earlier, infant Roland had sat in his swing chair and observed his three-year-old brother Parker perform the same manipulation with the broom. Becoming ambulatory, he was now able to do what he had been wanting to do since he was six months old. The interesting thing is that Roland has never shown any interest in the broom since then. He was finally able to satisfy his curiosity, and that was enough.

I could tell you of a dozen such episodes that I observed during the first week that Roland was walking. Clearly, he had stored up a database of "must do when able" deeds and was simply awaiting his moment of mobility. His siblings had been "teaching" him what was fun, what was important, and what he could do as soon as he could walk. He had learned from observation that when Daddy came home, it was wonderful: Mama was happy, Gracie was happy, Laila was happy, and Parker Man was REALLY happy, so Roland was happy too.

This is an important observation. The oldest child learns from Mama that Daddy is very important to everyone's welfare and happiness. Once the honoring-Daddy ball is rolling, half of the goal is reached. Honor given to Daddy has positive repercussions toward Mama. Likewise, dishonor breeds dishonor. Nervousness and fear breed nervousness and fear. Unhappiness produces unhappiness. Forfeited ground is hard to recover.

Training a child is life training. It doesn't mean just discipline, education, or academics.

Training a child is life training. It doesn't mean just discipline, education, or academics. Training is communication and example pertaining to all of life's experiences: to count as you go up and down steps, to obey the first time, to learn to read by being read to, to make a peanut butter sandwich by watching or helping, to learn to work on a motorcycle by seeing Daddy do it, and a million other things. Effective training is happening all the time in a properly managed home. But negative training happens constantly as well—by observation of anger; by lack of participation; by rejection, indifference, and boredom; by stern, forced school lessons—sitting at the table while Mama scowls; and last but certainly the most powerful negative training of all, by the master of all life training—the TV.

There are several lessons from this study of Roland that I hope to pass along to my readers. The first is that books I read 40 years ago are still helping me be a good teacher/trainer/thrilling person who makes my grandkids' lives exciting, so I would suggest that they are worth the read. Keep in mind that it was not so much the word cards that transformed my thinking; it was the fact that my baby's brain was on a fast track of learning, as the things I poured into her brain would provide the foundation for a lifetime of satisfying learning.

The next thing to learn from the Roland study is this: Your baby is bored. Your baby's toys are boring. Your baby's mind needs to be challenged, occupied, and stimulated. Your baby wants real-life objects, not plastic toys; she wants to see what you are doing, feel what you are stirring, smell it, and taste it. If you are cooking, set your baby in a prop-up chair of some kind where he or she can watch, and then talk through your project. Let your babies be part of real life.

What's This?

What really got my mind focused on the Roland study was something that happened during a shopping trip. Shoshanna (our youngest daughter) and I were checking out at Costco. She was holding her 27-month-old baby, Penelope. Unexpectedly the cashier stopped, looked straight at Penelope, held up a cucumber and asked, "What's this?" Penelope's little tongue twisted as she worked to utter the new word, "Cucumber." We were all surprised and laughed. Then the lady held up an onion, followed by all the different vegetables in the purchase, asking the name of each one, "What's this?" Without mistake, that tiny tot named lettuce, cabbage, carrots, different kinds of melons, garlic, different kinds of peppers, bananas, mango, pineapple, coconut, potatoes, corn, etc. She knew them all, although she had to work hard to pronounce the new words. Everyone nearby had turned their attention to watch this baby call out the correct answers.

I later asked Shoshanna when she had taught Penelope these words, and she looked as surprised as I was. She said, "Well, we eat a lot of fresh foods, and I often give her a choice of fruits or veggies, but…I guess she knows it because we just talk to her as if she knows things. We just never stopped to question her, and I am sure this is the first time she has pronounced most of them."

Does Penelope have an unfair advantage in life? You bet she does! Did it come from being sent off on a school bus for early Head Start kindergarten? NO! (Just so you will know, it is now on public record that Head Start children have a much poorer grade average than children who start school later. This type of artificial classroom education is NOT successful at school or at home.)

254

College By Twelve

Perhaps you have seen the famous Harding family on TV. The family's first six children have all started college by age 12, which makes them rather unusual. Their daughter became the youngest medical doctor ever in the US. As I read their literature and studied their interviews, I tried to wrap my mind around the big questions everyone was asking them: "WHY are your children able to do this? HOW did you homeschool them to be able to do this? Are you as parents brilliant?"

When a baby is observing and participating in what others are doing, that child's mind is creating building blocks that will set him apart for life. I have met the parents and listened to them speak. They seem totally normal, and so do their children. What jumped out to me, as I read their book and watched the interviews, was something that occurred by happenstance. Mr. Harding was studying calculus for a college class when his first child was just four years old. His wife worked in the evenings, so he would babysit. In order to study without constant interruptions and to keep the little one happy, he pretended that she was a fellow student. She sat at the table with him as he read her the questions, discussed the problems, and gave her the answers. For hours every night, their study occupied her and kept her happy, because Daddy was making her the center of his attention. Little Hannah became a serious mathematician before she turned 12 years old. At the time, it never occurred to Daddy that it was setting a precedent for the rest of her life, and the lives of all her siblings.

The Key of the Roland Study

The crux of everything I learned through my observation of Roland is that when a baby is observing and participating in what others are doing, that child's mind is creating building blocks that will set him apart for life. A child who sees a daddy and mama laugh and rejoice, pray and show thankfulness, study and learn, teach adults the Bible, etc., will grow up with this ingrained into his soul. A child sitting at your feet while you teach Romans to a room full of adults is becoming a Bible teacher. Our son Nathan, who sat at his daddy's feet while Daddy taught Romans, says that the logic of that book shapes almost everything he does in life.

Music Gifts

Musical families help drive home this concept. It is standard knowledge that musical families usually produce musically gifted children. People who love music play, sing, and listen to music all the time; it is just a part of life. There are several interesting studies showing that children adopted into musically gifted families are also musically gifted, although their biological history would not indicate this.

The question has to be asked in regard to any person's gift, talent, ability, or even intelligence: Is it biological, or could the greater part of this person's extraordinary ability come from very early opportunity? I believe that it is both: genetic make-up can bestow gifts, and early opportunities build into a baby's mind the material to set that child apart for the rest of his life.

The Leaders of the Pack

Parents hold in their hands their children's future success, not by giving them advanced education as children or teens, but by giving them the opportunity of observation and participation in a joyful, productive life as soon as they are born. It is not piles of workbooks that will make your children the leaders of the pack; it is your holding them on your hip, talking to them like they can understand everything you say and do. From day one, treat them like they are your best buddies with whom you want to share every good thing that comes your way. Treat them like fellow believers, sharing prayer, the Word, concern, victory, and praise, and they will love Christ from their youth and never turn away.

Greater Expectations
by Debi Pearl

What makes some people seem to soar, excited to learn, to grow, to take on one challenge after another and still be capable of more? What makes a person so satisfied and enthusiastic about life that he wants to share his knowledge with everyone, knowing he has something worth sharing? How can you take your children to that place? For that matter, how can you get there yourself?

God did not design us to idle away in endless boredom with no challenges, waiting for life to happen. Nor are we designed to exist in a state of distraction, always being entertained. We were not created to live like pigs in self-indulgence. God expects more from his creation. There is no joy or satisfaction apart from personal growth, fulfilling the yearning to know. God instilled in us the drive to excel.

Life is best in the pursuit of knowledge and wisdom, in sharing what we learn, in hopes and dreams, and a struggle to overcome. Winners feel better than losers, and God created us to win—not in a contest with others, but in our struggle against the world, the flesh, and the devil, against the demons of doubt, ignorance, and inaction. As we strive to know, we will grow. This brings glory to the One in whose image we are created, and it prepares us to be worthy and interesting sons and daughters in His coming kingdom.

We should be constantly stimulated with possibilities. Man performs best when focused and committed. How can I build a better boat, construct a more effective website, write a better musical, or win the world to Christ? Perhaps I shall do it all! Ah, but when a couple shares a dream and the burden of making that dream come true, they are functioning in the highest calling. When the entire family—with all the children—shares the pursuit of a vision, it grows the children into strong leaders. This is what sets some families apart from all others—a vision, a purpose, and a willingness to work together to realize something greater than themselves.

The truly successful family shares a dream and pours its combined energies into making it reality. I have observed families excel in this regard. No one had to tell them they needed a dream; it was just a natural part of their makeup. I know other families that have raised well-educated but useless daughters and weak men who lacked confidence. Both extremes were sincere and wanted what was best for their children, but one family invested their talents while another buried them out of fear.

Children's success starts with Mom and Dad. It starts with the parent (one or both) ready to lead the charge. Most things are more easily caught than taught. Living a life with vision is one of those things that must be caught. A child can catch small visions from a friend, a pastor, or another kid, but vision comes most readily when parents take the little guys by the hand and say, "See? Isn't this neat?"

The truly successful family shares a dream and pours its combined energies into making it reality.

A child who is immersed in the adventures of firsthand learning will be less self-centered and more interested in the world around him. A child left to himself is inclined to be silly, self-conscious, and have feelings of inferiority. Knowledge—real, firsthand knowledge that says, "I know because I experienced that"—imparts power and confidence and a greater desire to learn and share.

Today's child is prodded out of his warm bed and told to dress for school. He is fed a bowl of sugared cereal and loaded into a vehicle. At school, he is just one of the herd; he sits in a row, stands in a line, and plays on asphalt with all the other sad, bored kids. When he gets home in the afternoon, he sits in front of a screen in a dumbed-down state, watching some other kid sing, dance, have an adventure, or do something interesting or heroic. He feels himself to be the guy outside looking in through the window. The wonder in his soul lies dormant; he FEELS that life happens to the cool kids. Adventure is not his. He never considers that he might hold a tiny frog in his hand; he can't conceive that he might watch a snake slowly swallow a mouse. All he knows are the animals at the zoo boringly observing him observing them. It is a freeze-frame experience. Most children live regulated, packaged lives, never feeling the awe of the moment. Their young life is spent "killing time" and trying to stay out of trouble.

Children need an environment that stimulates the natural wonder in their souls.

They need time to investigate, play in the mud, share a song, and dream a dream.

Wonder is as close as a flushing toilet. I remember the day our grandson Laife flushed our commode for the first time. I pulled the top off the water closet and showed him how the chain pulled the small plug out of the hole at the bottom, allowing the water to rush into the toilet. He seriously studied the whole workings and manipulated the mechanism, his mind captivated with the construction and flow of water. He wanted to go outside to where the septic tank lay deep in the ground. Every day, every occasion, every new thing should be squeezed for all you can get out of it. Children need to know why, how, what, and they need to participate.

The sad fact is that many moms live in a fog of nothingness. They lead halfway lives. They halfheartedly homeschool the kids while they intermittently scan their Facebook page, reading and writing useless messages for people they don't even know. These moms are trapped in a net of daily boredom, so they have little interest in unearthing the unknown. It is a continuation of their youth— still killing time. They experience nothing to share with their children.

Hey, Mom, you were created to reflect God! It's time to start living with eternity in your eyes. You can't impart a vision to your sons and daughters unless you have one yourself.

As eternal beings, we were not designed to function in an endlessly boring, non-challenging daily life—kids included. Nor were we designed to exist in a state of entertained distraction— kids ESPECIALLY. God put into us a yearning to grow to be like him, to learn, to discover, to share, to plan, and to struggle to make our vision come true. He made us with a desire to rise above the mundane. We were designed after God's nature, in his image; to be like him and to be his friend. We were not meant to just survive. Every one of us—man, woman, and child— can be satisfied only by living on the cutting edge of discovery.

Bobbie Sue's Book List...
Homeschool/Parenting

- **A Christian Manifesto** by Dr. Francis Schaeffer, Crossway books.
- **All the Way Home** by Mary Pride.
- **Better Late than Early and The Successful Homeschool Family Handbook** by Raymond and Dorothy Moore.
- **Beyond Survival: A guide to Abundant Life Homeschooling** by Diana Waring.
- **Child Training Tips** by Reb Bradley.
- **For the Children's Sake** by Susan Schaeffer MacCaulay.
- **Going Home to School** by Llewellyn B. Davis, The Elijah Company.
- **High School Handbook** by Mary Schofield, CHEA.
- **Hints on Child Training** by H. Clay Trumbull.
- **Home Schooling and the Law** by Michael Farris, HSLDA.
- **Homeschooling for Eternity** by Skeet Savage.
- **Full Time parenting: A Guide to Family Based Discipleship** and **Homeschooling From a Biblical Worldview** by Israel Wayne.
- **Honey for a Child's Heart** by Gladys Hunt, Zondervan.

Gladys Hunt
HONEY FOR A child's heart
The Imaginative Use of Books in Family Life
Fourth Edition
Annotated List of Books for Ages 0-14

ISRAEL WAYNE
Full-Time PARENTING
A GUIDE TO FAMILY-BASED DISCIPLESHIP

- **Is Public Education Necessary?** by Samuel Blumenfeld, Devin-Adair.
- **Senior High: A Home Designed Form+U+La** by Barbara Edtl Shelton.
- **Shepherding a Child's Heart** and **Instructing a Child's Heart** by Tedd Tripp.
- **Books by Ruth Beechick**
  - Teaching Primaries
  - Teaching Juniors
  - You Can Teach Your Child Successfully
  - A Home Start in Reading
  - An Easy Start in Arithmetic
  - A Strong Start in Language

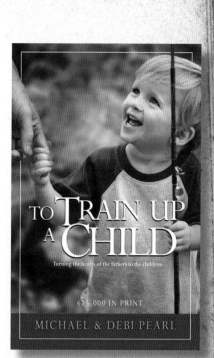

- **The Christian Home School** by Gregg Harris.
- **The Hurried Child** by David Elkind.
- **The Second American Revolution** by John Whitehead.
- **To Train Up a Child** by Michael & Debi Pearl.
- **Jumping Ship** by Michael & Debi Pearl.
- **What the Bible Says About Child Training** by Richard Fugate.
- **When You Rise Up: A Conventional Approach to Homeschooling** by R.C. Sproul.
- **Raising Godly Children in an Ungodly World** by Ken & Steve Ham.
- **Already Gone** by Ken Ham & Britt Beemer.
- **Already Compromised** by Ken Ham & Greg Hall.
- **Moms Who Changed The World** by Lindsay O'Conner.

nogreaterjoy.org

No Greater Joy   iMissionaries   Good and Evil   CreatedtobehisHelpmeet   Preparingto...hisHelpmeet   `Bulk Herb S

No Greater Joy Ministries – Family Magazine, Child Training Articles, Marriage Resources, Bible Teaching Videos from...

Search   Websites and Resources

Websites and Resources for Learning Styles and Homeschooling

Just starting homeschooling or are you thinking about it? These resources help you through the huge array of curriculum and resources available.

- **EHO Lite**
  This person has done all the work for you. She put her chidren's assignments online. (so they can do them independently; they will also be saved for her younger siblings.) Grade levels and courses include 180 days of homeschool lessons. Assignments cover reading, writing, grammar, spelling, vocabulary, math, history, social studies, geography, science, Bible, computer, music, art, PE, health, and logic. All available free at http://www.eho.org/

- **All in One Homeschool**
  This site lists subjects and then breaks them down into categories. Includes links for free print outs and resources. I REALLY liked it. http://allinonehomeschool.com/

- **A2Z Home's Cool**
  http://homeschooling.gomilpitas.com/directory/Sciences.htm#.UXFVoqKsh8F

- **Enchanted Learning**
  This site was mentioned by many people and seems to cover every subject. http://www.enchantedlearning.com/Home.html

- **Ambleside Online**
  Free curriculum designed to be as close as possible to Charlotte Mason's method. http://www.amblesideonline.org/index2.shtml

- **Charlotte Mason Method**
  Children are taught as whole persons through a wide range of interesting living books, firsthand experiences, and good habits. http://simplycharlottemason.com/basics/what-is-the-charlotte-mason-method/

- **World Fashion Education**
  Directory of free homeschool curricula, literature, and text books organized for the use of homeschooling families. http://www.oldfashionededucation.com/
- **Donna Young's resources and printables.**
  This site is written and maintained by a career homeschooling mother. All kinds of topics are available listed by subject. http://donnayoung.org/
- **Lesson Pathways**
  Free curriculum for K-5 grades. http://www.lessonpathways.com/
- **Ron Paul Curriculum**
  Students learn the basics of western civilization and liberty; how it was won, how it is being lost, and how it will be restored. Get free courses that cover free market economics and government, plus a how-to course on reclaiming America, one county at a time. Mathematics, Earth Science, Biology, Chemistry, and Physics; its all covered, and when completed, the curriculum's first six years of instructional videos and course materials will be free online. http://www.ronpaulcurriculum.com/public/main.cfm
- **Brainpop**
  Information and videos covering many subjects to instruct your child. http://www.brainpop.com/
- **Education.com**
  This website is not from a Christian perspective, so use with caution. It does have some good activates and projects divided by grade levels. http://www.education.com/
- **The Christian Home School Hub**
  Began as a small idea by founder Lynda Ackert. As a homeschooling mom, she wanted a place where she could connect with other Christian homeschooling parents and share resources. http://www.christianhomeschoolhub.spruz.com/about-us.htm
- **School Express**
  This website has a lot of worksheets that can be printed. They charge a yearly fee and it is not a Christian site. http://www.schoolexpress.com/

Gabriel's
Point
Work Ethic

Pearl Kid #2

One thing in my training that has proved invaluable to me is a strong work ethic. I want to pass this gift on to my children, so I have done much reflection on how I was trained to work. Many homeschool young men have missed this critical training. Homeschool families are often so caught up with "doing curriculum" that they miss this vital element of life's assignments. Traditional schooling is mostly 10,000 boring hours of useless facts crammed into a curriculum. Much of what is "learned" is quickly forgotten because it was irrelevant.

I remember that from the time I was 10 until I reached 18 years of age, we would complete our school in the morning, and in the afternoon we worked. Work wasn't just mindless exertion; it was a time of learning. The skills I learned while working as a young boy are the same skills I use today. These skills are just as important, or maybe more so, than the information I learned while sitting in the house "doing homeschooling" in the mornings. It was the work ethic (not the schoolwork) I learned as a boy that has made me who I am today. It didn't matter whether we were planting, hoeing, picking, and packing tomatoes for a living or selling books online; we children knew that we were an important part of the work of the family. Working with our parents gave us a real sense of personal accomplishment and a broad vision of what was possible.

In my mid-teens, Dad was wise enough to allow me to hire on with one of the carpenters (Tim) in our church. This gave me the opportunity to learn different trades and to be on the job with other honorable, hardworking men. In order to keep work interesting, Tim would continually provoke us to use our brains. He would drill us on all kinds of facts, from geography to science to music. He turned everything into a contest, which caused me to love quizzes and questions. His constant interrogation created in me a powerful hunger to learn. To know the name of a river in Russia or the height of the highest peak in China, when Tim did NOT know it, was exhilarating. To figure in my head the correct rafter length before he could figure it on the calculator was a real victory. Now, as an adult, I realize that Tim pushed me, not only into learning facts, but into the love of knowledge, all the while teaching me how to make a respectful living with my hands. It was the ultimate classroom.

So, Lori and I also are committed to teach our children to put feet to the knowledge they will accumulate over the years of their childhood. They will not be ignorant of book learning, and just as important, they will not be ignorant of life. And, perhaps best of all, they will be mentally and emotionally equipped to work in a creative manner, enjoying all the challenges of life that God sends their way.

One thing in training that has proved invaluable to me is a strong work ethic.

—Gabriel Pearl

Curriculum

The year we started homeschooling our budget for supplies was $0 and I wondered how I would do it. Someone mentioned me on social networking and suddenly older moms started offering me all their leftover "little kid" stuff. You really, really don't need much they all said...but it was so much fun for me and the children to go through the boxes of all that awesome stuff! From that moment I knew I wanted to be a homeschooler, I wanted to be just like those generous, encouraging, homeschooling moms.

Blogs and Resources for Homeschooling on pages 274-275

Websites and Resources for Curriculm found on pages 276-277

Which Curriculum is the Best?
by Rebekah (Pearl) Anast

When parents decide to homeschool, one of the first questions raised in their minds is "which curriculum?" There are some wonderful lines of material out there for the home-schooled kid of every grade and bent. How to choose one? Your homeschooling friend from the church says such-and-such worked better for her son than anything else, and she has tried a score of options. The magazines you read are advertising the most up-and-coming curriculum available. And then, there is your budget to consider… What if you choose a lemon and put your kid and yourself through misery for the next 10 months?

Good question.

I have not seen or sampled very many curricula. As a student, I used very little, but what I did use was a mixture of A Beka and A.C.E. paces. I don't believe either one of them were tailored to meet my needs as a student. But I have no fear about choosing the correct curriculum for my children. You see, it's not a question of what type of curriculum, but rather, what type of child.

Curious George Learns the Alphabet, flash cards, cassette tapes, and schoolbooks were my first approach to teaching Joe Courage his A-B-Cs. He was learning at a moderate pace, I suppose, but not with the lightning speed and enthusiasm he shows in other areas of life. I wondered why. An unplanned trip to Walgreen's with Joe was what I needed.

We strolled down the crowded aisle, looking for a broom, and discovered a section of coffee table entertainment. Puzzles of all kinds, including 3D puzzles of cars and trucks, a map of the United States, and even a couple of children's puzzles of numbers and alphabet pieces. We bought them all and spent less than twenty bucks. The first time Joe tried to put the alphabet puzzle together, he got frustrated and stomped on the pieces. His reaction was so violent that I was amazed. He was duly spanked, but the intensity of his emotions toward the puzzle clued me in: Joe has a "hands-on" brain.

Within twenty-four hours, he could put the puzzle together in a matter of minutes. He had tried and retried a hundred times without prompting. He would not rest until he had it figured out. Not only would he repeat the process again and again, Joe would hold each piece up and ask me what it was – or guess. "Is this M for mama?" I had to be fast in my response, because he was not going to wait around for me to reply; two seconds later there was another piece in his hand. A couple of days later, he was able to put the puzzle together while naming the letters and sounds to himself. "A is for a-a-alligator, B is for b-b-bear, C is for c-c-cookie, D is for d-d-daddy…" And that was the curriculum that Joe used to teach himself the alphabet.

Sight, Hearing, and Touch

You are probably already familiar with the three methods of learning: Sight, Hearing, and Touch. Almost everyone has at some time or other diagnosed themselves by saying, "Oh, I learn best by seeing something done…" or "I need to read it for myself; you're not making sense…"

Ever wonder why some people prefer a map, while others do just fine following verbal directions? Why do some people read instruction manuals and information books while others prefer fiction for entertainment and seminars for learning? Aha!

The light has gone on in your brain. Yes—your child learns in a different way from others. Some may learn well with a good mixture of two, or even all three methods, but many will prefer one single method of learning.

Actions Speak Louder

Joseph Courage is a hands-on learner. He needs action and touch. Joe needs to be physically involved in the lessons he is learning. He likes to work, play, sing, and talk his way through "schoolwork." This manner of learning may be the most difficult for the average teacher to work with. Hands-on teaching requires enormous creativity and involvement. There are not many curricula that can meet this learning bent, unless they are project suggestion books and a series of games. There may be such a one out there, but I am not aware of it. I had a sister and a brother who learned this way. I believe my Mom is also a hands-on learner, thus her manner of teaching was more hands-on and creative than it otherwise would have been.

When I was a child, one of my Mom's most used teaching tools was peanut butter "play-dough." She made it regularly and kept plastic containers full of decorating supplies (peanuts, raisins, M&Ms) on hand. We crowded around the table and created all kinds of things, only to eat them in the end. Almost every kid has eaten play-dough, but we did it legally and safely.

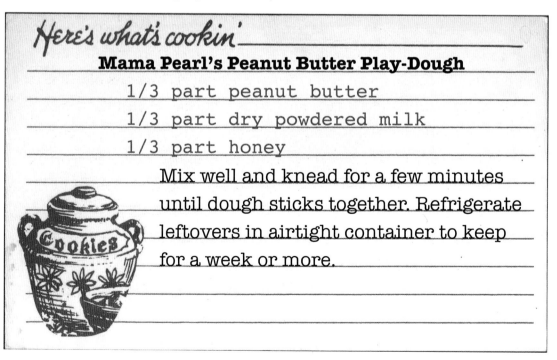

Here's what's cookin'

Mama Pearl's Peanut Butter Play-Dough

1/3 part peanut butter

1/3 part dry powdered milk

1/3 part honey

Mix well and knead for a few minutes until dough sticks together. Refrigerate leftovers in airtight container to keep for a week or more.

Another method Mom used was the Math-It games which we bought from the Moore Foundation (moorefoundation.com or 800-891-5255). Also, for math we counted change, and had "business" over the kitchen table, buying and selling snack goods to each other. We played games that involved a lot of vocabulary, history, and facts. We learned to read by taking turns reading aloud behind an imaginary pulpit, making our voices carry and our words clear for the "audience" of four siblings and two parents. The critics were very strict.

Mom had project after project going for her own interest, from mushroom farming to making natural dyes. She read the instructions, but preferred to try things herself, and still does. We learned from her projects as well.

I think one of the best curricula for a hands-on learner is to work with someone. My brother Gabriel learned an immense amount from working on construction sites with other men from the time he was twelve years old. The conversation and practical skills he acquired on the job-site opened the door of knowledge for him, and showed him how to "teach" himself. Finding a genre of knowledge and a "teacher" you trust may be difficult, but it is definitely worth a careful look. A girl could work at a fabric store, flower shop, milk farm, novelty shop, restaurant, with a mid-wife, etc… A boy could work with a black-smith, carpenter, veterinarian, businessman, etc… So much is learned by working at a job: knowledge, discipline, confidence, social interaction, and much more.

As an aside, the famous Robert Kiyosaki, who wrote the book, Rich Dad, Poor Dad, recommended that before anyone starts a business, they should get a job working for a small company and "work through" all the jobs in the company they can in order to get a well-rounded business education. I would safely guess that Robert Kiyosaki is a hands-on learner.

Godspeed with your hands-on student!

Ears to Hear

Very few children will turn away from some project or game that requires their physical involvement. However, not all children prefer to learn by the hands-on method. The hearing-learner will be impatient with the process and want you to "just tell me…" so they can get on with life. I am this way.

When I was a young student, games and projects were fun, but not in conjunction with learning. If I wanted to learn something, I wanted to be told how to do it, succinctly and articulately. Then I wanted my teacher to get out of my way and let me at it. Games and projects slowed me down and bored my mind; reading instructions was loathsome. I loved to memorize by listening to tapes or learning songs.

Mom made a series of cassette tapes accompanied by charts that taught phonics, and I can still remember them clearly. I would have preferred doing school entirely by audio tape or with a classroom teacher, and would have learned twice as much, twice as fast if that had been my sole manner of instructional input.

Even today, I have trouble reading directions. The page just goes blank when I look at it. I buy patterns (rarely) only to study the pictures and sew what "looks like it." I rarely fail in this method. "A picture is worth a thousand words" is a true statement; seeing a picture is just like hearing something explained. Words on paper are not anywhere near the same as a spoken word.

Homeschool videos were not around when I needed them. I have no doubt I would have preferred teaching videos over any other method of learning.

If you have a hearing-learner, reading aloud to them

is a great way to start. Mom began to read aloud to me when I was tiny, and she claims that I was reading by the time I turned four. Even now, at thirty years old, when I think of a word, I can hear it said in my mind. When I spell a difficult word, I do so by remembering it being spelled aloud. I learned to spell Wednesday by hearing someone pronounce it "Wed-nes-day" slowly for me.

I still know my multiplication tables, because Mom chanted them aloud to me, and had me chant them back to her. Chanting the "times tables" drove my brother crazy, but for me there was no other way. I enjoy reading, but I learn better from books that are written in a conversational style, rather than those that are written in instructional form.

If your child finds it easier to learn with videos and tape curriculum, audited classes, songs and chant repetitions, and all other things taught by the hearing method, then it will be obvious to you what curricula to use for that student. If he or she is like me, hearing will open the door of ability to read for themselves. Once they can "hear" a word in their head when they see it, they will soon become "self-taught."

Eye of the Beholder

This may be the most convenient type of student for parents to teach. Thankful are the teachers who have students who prefer to read the information for themselves!

My sister Shalom learns best by sight. In her case, a project was overwhelming and verbal instructions were either too fast or too slow. She had no patience with being told the teacher's perceptions. Her mentality was, "it doesn't matter what you know; give me the book, and soon I'll know it."

Shalom spent hours in her room, surrounded by stacks of books that she studied with the patience of a sea turtle. The rest of us would walk by her door and peer in occasionally, simply amazed at her willingness to stay pinned to her desk. To force Shalom to study in a manner that was not comfortable to her was completely fruitless. She would sit through instructions and videos and family games, only to retire to her room to stay up all night studying and reading to learn what she needed to know. If Shalom ran out of books, her life was without form and void until she replenished the storehouse. Her walls and ceiling were lined with charts, maps, and posters of every sort.

It is important for a sight-learner to know how to find written information. My husband is a sight-learner as well. He could not survive on this planet without the World Wide Web. Everything he wants to know is available to him by typing in a small command. For the sight-learner, such a tool is almost miraculous. There is no limit to what he/she can learn if the ability to find knowledge is given to them. A local library offers the same type of resource. But, even in the library, a child needs to know how to look and where to look in order to find the books he needs.

Not only do sight-learners need to read instructional books, they need demonstrations as well. If your sight-learner is interested in medical topics, they will enjoy watching surgeries, births, and medical procedures in person, as well as on video. Seeing it done will give them the confidence that they can do it themselves. The smallest children need to be lifted up high to watch mama or daddy perform the simple functions of life in the household. "Look, this is how you wash dishes…" "This is how you count money…" "This is the way you comb your hair…" Show-and-tell should be the teacher's way of life for a sight-learner.

Math problems, at times, will need to be solved on the white board step by step, but do so in a very visual manner. Spelling words will need to be on paper as well. Diagrams and graphs will make sense to a sight learner, where they might look more like ancient Egyptian hieroglyphics to other children.

And remember, if your sight-learner asks you to "show me," what he/she really means is, "I need to see it done."

What Now?

I believe that all three of these methods of learning are likely to be found in your household. One child may need two methods to learn at their highest potential, and you might be completely different from that child. Experiment by teaching them something three different ways, and see which method seems to "ring a bell" with your student. Once you know how they learn, choosing a curriculum will be much easier and safer. You might discover that pieces of two different curricula are what you need for one child, whereas another single curriculum might meet your second child's needs entirely. If your best friend recommends what works for her, find out how her child learns before you invest a year's savings in learning material that works great for someone else.

And, if you are one of those teachers or students who has been badly burned by a curriculum that just didn't take, take heart and let your hope return! You are not necessarily a poor teacher or a poor learner; you probably just need a new approach. Now you are much better equipped to find it!

Bobbie Sue's List of...
Blogs and Resources

- **Home School Legal Defense Association**

  A nonprofit advocacy organization established to defend and advance the constitutional right of parents to direct the education of their children and to protect family freedoms. Through annual memberships, HSLDA is tens of thousands of families united in service together providing a strong voice when and where needed.

  http://www.hslda.org/about/

- **Safe Eyes**

  I highly encourage you to get internet protection on your computer. Safe Eyes is the program that we recommend.

  http://www.internetsafety.com/

- **Library and Educational Services**

  If you are looking for a source to buy Christian books at a greatly reduced price then you will want to check out this site.

  http://www.libraryanded.com/

- **State-specific Resources**

  This site has a map that you can click on, or use the pull-down menu to find your state-specific resources.

  http://holtmcdougal.hmhco.com/hm/state/map.htm

- **Holy Spirit Homeschooling**

  This blog is loaded with advice on how to run a business at home while homeschooling. http://www.holyspiritledhomeschooling.net/

- **Homeschool Mosaics**

  Loaded with all kinds of info about the many different ways to homeschool.http://homeschoolmosaics.com/

- **Heart of Wisdom**

  Curriculum strong in History, Science, and Character. All of their books use the Bible as the foundation.

  http://www.heartofwisdom.com/homeschoollinks/category/faqs/

- **Curriculum Resource Directory**

  http://www.angelfire.com/mo/sassafrassgrove/
- **Homeschool Diaries**

  An encouraging website to help you explain to people what you do, and why you do it. **http://www.homeschooldiaries.com/**
- **Homeschooling Wisconisn**

  A place of refreshment and encouragement on your unique homeschool journey. This website provides homeschool parents with daily spiritual nourishment and guidance. **http://www.homeschoolingwisconsin.com/**
- **Free Homeschool Ideas**

  This site offers lot's of free resources from daily deals to printable math sheets. **http://www.freehomeschooldeals.com/**
- **Sheri Graham**

  As a homeschool mother of five children, Sheri's desire is to provide resources and encouragement for the Christian family. Her website is full of FREE articles and downloads, eBooks, homeschooling information, recipes, and more.

  http://sherigraham.com/homeschool
- **The Potter's Hand Academy**

  Some homeschooling families avoid the use of textbooks because of fear that using them will make school dry and boring. That does not have to be the case at all! There are some advantages to homeschooling using the textbook method. **http://www.thepottershandacademy.com/**
- **The Perkins Family Homepage**

  The Christian family needs a harbor in cyberspace that is designed with them in mind. Children need access to the internet without fear of stumbling upon offensive or inappropriate material. Parents need web sites that will encourage them in their walk with the Lord.

  http://www.geocities.com/~perkinshome/index.html

No Greater Joy Ministries – Family Magazine, Child Training Articles

nogreaterjoy.org

No Greater Joy   iMissionaries   Good and Evil   CreatedtobehisHelpmeet   Preparingto...hisHelpmeet   Bulk Herb Sto

No Greater Joy Ministries – Family Magazine, Child Training Articles, Marriage Resources, Bible Teaching Videos from...

Search   Websites and Resources

Curriculum Resources

- **Schoolhouse Teachers**
  Need a little help with teaching? Sign your children up for one or more subjects and get online instruction from these teachers. http://schoolhouseteachers.com/
- **Used Curriculm Resources**
  http://www.angelfire.com/mo/sasschool/misc2.html
- **HSLDA**
  Curriculum list from HSLDA http://www.hslda.org/highschool/curriculum.asp
- **A Beka Books**
  http://www.abeka.com/HomeSchool/
- **Alpha Omega Publications**
  http://www.aophomeschooling.com/home/
- **Accelerated Christian Education (A.C.E.)**
  Utilizes the PACE system http://www.aceministries.com/
- **BJU Press**
  http://www.bjupresshomeschool.com/webapp/wcs/stores/servlet/home__
- **Christian Light Education**
  Curriculum covering kindgergarten through 12th grade.
  http://www.clp.org/christian_light_education
- **Classical Conversations**
  Combines the classical method of learning with a Biblical worldview.
  http://www.classicalconversations.com/common/cc-101
- **Cornerstone Curriculum**
  Teach children to stand, speak and restore. We must not pull back from society or try to blend in. We must equip our children to challenge the culture with the truth of Christianity and the life of Christ. http://www.cornerstonecurriculum.com/
- **Covenant Home Curriculum**
  Provides families with sound textual material base on the classical approach to education. Full-service programs are offered for children from pre-kindergarten through grade 12. http://www.covenanthome.com/
- **Notgrass Company**
  http://www.notgrass.com/notgrass/homeschool-curriculum-high-school/

- **Saxon Homeschool**
  Well known and popular curriculum. Keep in mind that they are not a Christian company. http://saxonhomeschool.hmhco.com/en/saxonhomeschool.htm
- **Bright Ideas Press**
  Illuminations is an all-inclusive curriculum, covering Bible, Language Arts (grammar, writing, copywork, spelling and vocabulary), Literature, Science, Humanities (poetry, theatre, music, and art), Geography, History, and Life Skills and Projects. Does not include math.
  https://www.brightideaspress.com/store/index.php?main_page=page&id=11
- **KONOS**
  Is about...one home schooler talking to another home schooler... sharing curriculum designed by two homeschooling moms for their own children. It's about sharing 24 years of homeschooling experience. It's about passing on a vision to build families that honor God. It's about instilling Godly character in the next generation. It's about building relationships between family members. It's about achieving excellence in education. It's about reading wide and deep. It's about recognizing "God put the wiggle in children, and we should not try to take it out." http://www.konos.com/www/
- **Mott Media**
  http://www.mottmedia.com/
- **Rod and Staff**
  Bible-based textbooks designed to make children God-conscious. This curriculum not only teaches the Bible but uses many illustrations of how Bible principles can be applied in everyday life. If your child struggles with math, we recommend R&S math.
  http://www.milestonebooks.com/list/Rod_and_Staff_Curriculum/
- **Sonlight**
  Provides complete Christian homeschool curriculum. With literature-rich, Christ-centered programs, your family is guaranteed to love learning together.
  http://www.sonlight.com/
- **Veritas Press**
  Specializes in providing educational materials for a classical Christian education in Christian schools and home schools. Whether it be phonics, studying the Bible, history, or the great books studied in the Omnibus Curriculum, you will be blessed in extraordinary ways by your use of Veritas materials. http://www.veritaspress.com/

Treasure Hunt!

See how many things you can find in this book.

How many keys?

How many tacks?

How many apples?

How many cars?

How many monarchs?

How many bells?

How many pennies?

How many blue ribbons?

How many slates?

How many whisks?

How many pencils?

How many tape measures?

How many tomatoes?

Don't forget about Debi's 2¢

Send us **your** best homeschooling ideas!